T0065548

BUILDING CULTURAL INTELLIGENCE in CHURCH and MINISTRY

10 Ways to Assess and Improve Your Cross-Cultural Competence in Church, Ministry and the Workplace

OSOBA O. OTAIGBE

authorHOUSE®

AuthorHouse™ UK
1663 Liberty Drive
Bloomington, IN 47403 USA
www.authorhouse.co.uk
Phone: 0800.197.4150

Published by AuthorHouse 07/26/2016

ISBN: 978-1-5246-2990-8 (sc)
ISBN: 978-1-5246-2988-5 (hc)
ISBN: 978-1-5246-2989-2 (e)

Print information available on the last page.

Any people depicted in stock imagery provided by Thinkstock are models,
and such images are being used for illustrative purposes only.
Certain stock imagery © Thinkstock.

This book is printed on acid-free paper.

Scripture quotations marked NIV are taken from the Holy Bible, New
International Version®. NIV®. Copyright © 1973, 1978, 1984 by International
Bible Society. Used by permission of Zondervan. All rights reserved.

Contents

Forewords vii

Dedication xiii

Acknowledgements xv

How To Use This Book xvii

Chapter 1   Introduction: Why Cultural Intelligence is
Important in Church and Ministry 1

Part 1

Cultural Intelligence Drive in Cross-Cultural Ministry, Mission and the Workplace

Chapter 2   Intrinsic Motivation in Cross-Cultural Church and
Ministry 15

Chapter 3   External (Extrinsic) Motivation in Cross-Cultural
Church and Ministry 24

Chapter 4   Competence and Confidence in Cross-Cultural
Church and Ministry 33

Part 2

Cultural Intelligence Knowledge in Cross-Cultural Ministry, Mission and the Workplace

Chapter 5   General Cultural Knowledge in Cross-Cultural
Church and Ministry 47

Chapter 6   Context-Specific Knowledge in Cross-Cultural
             Church and Ministry...60

                              Part 3

              Cultural Intelligence Strategy in Ministry,
                   Mission and the Workplace

Chapter 7   Strategic Planning in Cross-Cultural Church and
             Ministry...71

Chapter 8   Mindfulness in Cross-Cultural Church and Ministry...80

Chapter 9   Strategic Evaluation in Cross-Cultural Church and
             Ministry...88

                              Part 4

              Cultural Intelligence Action in Ministry,
                   Mission and the Workplace

Chapter 10   Verbal Behaviour in Cross-Cultural Church and
             Ministry...97

Chapter 11   Nonverbal Communication in Cross-Cultural
             Church and Ministry...104

Chapter 12   Recapping Church and Ministry plus Cultural
             Intelligence..111

About the Author 117

Bibliography 119

Forewords

Osoba's detailed treatment of Cultural Intelligence (CQ) raises awareness for the uninitiated by highlighting the constituent elements that serve as prerequisites for cultivating CQ. It should be noted that Osoba extends the definitional parameters of Cultural Intelligence to include organisational, denominational and subcultural interactions.

Of particular note, is the author's insightful scrutiny of the actions of several well-known biblical characters from a Cultural Intelligence vantage point. Osoba offers a fresh assessment of the activities of biblical luminaries such as Peter, Paul, David, Moses, Jonah, Esther, Ruth and Solomon - even to those of us who are already conversant with their life stories. Essentially, he spotlights these individuals (and the fictional character James Bond) to exemplify various aspects of CQ.

Osoba's compelling case for the development of Cultural Intelligence within the church community is perhaps encapsulated in his observation that: "when we interact with the Bible, we are in essence in a cross-cultural setting". As such, he notes that the cross-cultural spread of the Gospel message was initiated by the Holy Spirit. In this regard, Osoba's assessment serves to remind us that the need for cross-cultural proficiency is not a 21st century initiative!

Osoba gives consideration to several aspects of CQ including the role of mindfulness, values, and non-verbal communication. He additionally provides a list of helpful suggestions for improving general cultural knowledge and further offers suggestions for how CQ can be adopted and/or practised. Overall, the book is a useful tool for any individual, team, group or church community. Each section of the book contains a set of relevant and thought-provoking questions which should provide sufficient incentive for action to be taken beyond the realms of 'wishful thinking'.

Osoba proposes that the book is used as the underpinning element of a campaign strategy to facilitate "transformation into a cross-culturally competent church and Christian community". Alongside the support offered by Osoba and his team, the book has the potential to act as a catalyst to the body of Christ on this important issue. In short, it can be used to instigate the incremental and monumental shifts that form the bedrock of transformation.

Ultimately, this book supports the acquisition of the Cultural Intelligence that is essential for not only living within increasingly culturally diverse communities, but also necessary for the fulfilment of the Great Commission given to the Church.

Sharon Nugent, Learning and Development Officer, Discipleship and Ministries Network, The Methodist Church United Kingdom

Rev Osoba Otaigbe has written a comprehensive guide for helping the church more effectively relate and serve across cultural borders. Whether you're welcoming a community of refugees, travelling on a short-term mission experience, befriending an expat family, or simply interacting with an increasingly diverse society, this guide will help you love your neighbour. The book is packed full of insights about cultural intelligence and brings them to life for Christians. The case studies and discussion questions are particularly useful for making the theoretical ideas immensely practical. As both a cultural intelligence researcher and a Christian, it gives me great joy to commend Rev Osoba and his work to you.

David Livermore, PhD., author of Leading with Cultural Intelligence and President of Cultural Intelligence Centre USA

Commendations for Building Cultural Intelligence in Church and Ministry

Building Cultural intelligence in Church and Ministry is the finest resource I have read on the subject - Multicultural Intelligence. It is not only superbly written, but deeply theological and applicable to churches and businesses. As far as I am concerned it is a must -read for every Baptist Church. I would challenge any person to read this outstanding resource and not be challenged by its content. It is an accessible and highly thoughtful contribution to the field of multiculturalism.

Revd Wale Hudson-Roberts, Justice Enabler, Baptist Union of Great Britain

Rev Osoba's book on Cultural Intelligence in the Church and Ministry brings a unique cultural perspective that is often missing in studies on intercultural mission. He writes as an African pastor who leads and has had the experience of working in cultural diverse church and ministry in Britain. The book is certainly practitioner led offering case studies and questions for individuals and groups to consider as they journey on the road to cultural intelligence. This approach however does not mean lack of theological depth, as the reverse is the case combining multiple disciplines such as African theology, Social Science and Business Studies. Therefore the book is useful for both academic theologians and church practitioners who want to understand more about negotiating multiple cultures in what is an increasingly global culture.

Rev Israel Oluwole Olofinjana, Director, Centre for Missionaries from the Majority World, United Kingdom

Building Cultural Intelligence in Church and Ministry is a worthwhile work with important things to say and to give perceptive and practical guidance.

Prof. David Dunn-Wilson, Honorary Research Fellow, Cliff College, United Kingdom

We live in a Global Village where a lack of cultural intelligence limits Kingdom ventures and often divides communities. Osoba's book is a well researched, biblical, insightful and practical resource that will help us discern how we can better understand our own viewpoint and understand others perspectives. It's a must-read for any church leader working amongst different cultures.

Andy Frost, Director Share Jesus International, London United Kingdom

This is an interesting book with many fascinating insights that could only be shared in the way that Osoba has by someone who has travelled his road. I know from conversations with many who have travelled similar roads between cultures that 'culture' as 'the way we do things around here' has multiple layers that can feed into a common understanding when people like Osoba share as he has done.

What the book does so helpfully is to structure some of his personal insights into a book for study that can be experimented with and applied in diverse situations.

Revd. Richard Jackson, International Training Coordinator, Cliff College International Training Centre (CCITC)

In our rapidly changing society it is really important that we all develop greater cultural intelligence. If we are to become the vibrant Kingdom community of all nations that the Bible envisages we need much greater understanding and appreciation of those who are different from ourselves. This book, and the assessment and workshops that go alongside it, will be particularly helpful for leaders, churches and groups who want to grow in this area. Relating the concepts of cultural intelligence to passages of Scripture, it will certainly encourage some great discussion, learning and reflection for discipleship and mission

Revd Lynn Green, General Secretary, Baptist Union of Great Britain

More than ever, 'cultural intelligence' is a much-needed competence to grow, develop and nurture. Current fears and conflicts on the global and in local contexts, and not the least in churches, underscore this. Through this timely volume, Osoba O. Otaigbe brings his expertise as a cultural intelligence researcher, and years of experience working in cross-cultural and diverse contexts to offer an invaluable resource for churches. Building Cultural Intelligence in Church and Ministry draws on a variety of scholarly sources, biblical texts, and practical examples to provide readers with helpful insights and questions for reflection on developing cultural awareness, intelligence and competence. A welcome resource for ministerial/missional formation and both denominational and local church leadership!

Michael N. Jagessar (Revd Dr) Global and Intercultural Ministries, United Reformed Church (UK)

The Mission Jesus has called us to will never be achieved by remaining in our narrow cultural bunkers. I thank God for the Church, the family with which we have the privilege of praying 'our Father'. I thank God for the unity which recognises each other as brothers and sisters in Christ, but I also thank God for our amazing cultural diversity. We are not the same, we see things differently and often we misinterpret what we see and hear. For the great commission to be fulfilled, we need a church which not only acknowledges our cultural differences, but celebrates them – enriching our mission and recognising we need the whole church to reach the whole world with the good news of Jesus.

For the Evangelical Alliance, the emergence of our 'One People Commission' in 2010 (Directed by Pastor Yemi Adedeji) has profoundly influenced the culture and workings of the Alliance. I'm thankful to God for the new relationships and fresh ways of thinking and working. The Church from across the world is today helping to shape the 21st century Evangelical Alliance.

I trust that '*Building Cultural Intelligence in Church and Ministry*' will provide a valuable resource to the church in the UK and beyond.

Steve Clifford, General Director, Evangelical Alliance

What sets this book apart is that Rev Osoba Otaigbe practices what he has written. He faithfully lives out helping others live and work better together in our global world. His heart for helping others develop their cultural intelligence in practical ways makes this a must-read.

Julie Slagter, Manager, Certification & Client Services, Cultural Intelligence Centre USA

Dedication

This book is dedicated to Lase, Ofure and Oisejie

Acknowledgements

I'd like to thank God for giving me life and my family for their support throughout the writing of this book. I specially want to thank Anne Hurst for editing and proofreading the book several times, Dr Maureen Ayikoru for helping with the initial content editing, Dr David Livermore for reading through the materials and his valuable advice. I'd also like to thank members of our church, especially Janet Armor and Rosemarie Reid, who have been on this cross-cultural ministry journey with me. Thanks to the Pastor of Memorial Community Church, Revd. Mark Janes, Jill McWilliam and members for giving me the space to begin this cross-cultural ministry journey in the United Kingdom. Thanks also to all who have attended our workshops and those who have shared their stories and research on this subject with me during the writing of this book. I am grateful to Revd David Shosanya and Revd Kumar Rajagopalan for their support and giving me the space to serve London Baptist Churches. Special thanks to Revd Colin Marchant and Revd Phil Robinson for support and guidance during my studies and as newly accredited minister. I am very grateful to Andrew and Sarah Rogers for providing the much needed space to complete this book.

Finally I'd like to thank Revd Joe Kalpoyo, Revd Isreal Olofinjana, Revd David Ibiayo, Revd Steve Latham and Revd Father Victor Darlington for the times we met together to share on Culture and theology.

How can you assess and improve your cultural Intelligence for mission, ministry and the workplace?

Start with this book, take an online CQ assessment and attend one of our CQ workshops

For more details on how to run and order the cross-cultural competence campaign tool kit which includes online CQ self-assessment, workshop and small group video and book resources

Contact: Friendship Plus
osotaigbe@gmail.com or
Phone +447908109987

How To Use This Book

The purpose of this book is to enable individuals and churches to achieve local and global effectiveness in missions and ministries, through cultural intelligence audits, assessments, improvement, and strategic leadership development in a globalised world.

In a diverse city and world, we have so much in common, and we are also very different. We cannot all be the same; we are created by God in a very unique way. However, we do want to understand each other and work together effectively and peacefully to bring the Kingdom as proclaimed by Jesus to many in our city. Culture matters, whether national, ethnic, generational, organisational, or socio-economic. This book explores many themes within cultural intelligence. It can be used as a read-alone study guide, within small groups and mission groups. It can also be used as part of a campaign to build a culturally intelligent church by the power of the Holy Spirit. The word 'ministry' as used in this book refers to workplace, business and missions and "Cross-cultural" is used interchangeably with the word "Inter-cultural" in this book.

For working purposes, CQ means "Cultural Intelligence"

Mission, Ministry and the Workplace Plus Cultural Intelligence Campaign

We encourage every team, church, and group to use this book not only to improve their cultural intelligence, but also to carry out a campaign within their churches for maximum impact and transformation into a cross-culturally competent church and Christian community. The campaign involves working alongside our team. It begins by carrying out an individual and team cultural intelligence assessment. Secondly, we run a workshop to debrief the assessment report and discover how you can improve specific areas of your CQ. After the workshop, we follow up through coaching and mentoring, as the case may be. A final assessment is then taken to ascertain any improvement gained over the period.

When using this book in your small groups, we highly recommend getting the Work Book on Building Cultural intelligence in Church and Ministry and Video resource that accompanies our Church Cross-Cultural Competence Campaign Tool Kit. (CCCC Campaign Tool Kit)

Whether you are

> in a church that wants to connect with other cultures in your community;
> ministering in a very diverse congregation;
> in a ministry where you are reaching out to teenagers, young adults, and seniors;
> in a church with people from different organisational/ denominational church background;

or

> working in a cross-cultural workplace.

This book, together with the cultural intelligence online self-assessments, debriefing, and improvement workshops, is a helpful tool in increasing your cross-cultural competence in mission, ministry, and the workplace.

Expected Outcome after Using This Book and Attending One of Our Workshops

- More effective cross-cultural adaptability and decision-making
- Enhanced cross-cultural ministry and mission interactions

- Improved creativity and innovation in mission and ministry
- Improved/increased relationships within your congregation and wider community

Small Group and Individual Study Guide

Alternatively, you could decide to just use this book alone in your small groups and as a church. It is suitable for home groups, cell groups, leadership teams, and mission teams.

The method of campaign engagement is called **P.E.A.R.**

PREPARE

Assessments, self-assessments, or multi-rater assessments. To undertake the assessment, email: osotaigbe@gmail.com. For more details, visit www.ccsld.net and www.ccccampaign.com

ENGAGE

Workshops for debriefing of assessment report.

This one-day session will help you and your members assess, apply, and improve their cultural intelligence, which will enable them to engage with culturally diverse church members and people from other faiths (or those without a religion).

The session will include an introduction to the cultural intelligence model and research. Participants will be given examples and best practices for using cultural intelligence as they relate to worship and service within their local church and the wider community. At the end, participants will leave with an action plan for improving their cultural intelligence for missions and ministries.

We have a team that come and can run this workshop with you after or before you use this book.

APPLY

Small groups study using this book.

Coaching and mentoring on personal or group development plan that emerged during the workshop.

RESULTS

Result-based monitoring and final assessments to check the progress that has been made over the weeks or months since the campaign.

Chapter 1

Introduction: Why Cultural Intelligence Is Important in Church and Ministry

PREPARE

Paul the Roman Citizen

The crowd listened to Paul until he said this. Then they raised their voices and shouted, "Rid the earth of him! He's not fit to live!"

As they were shouting and throwing off their cloaks and flinging dust into the air, the commander ordered that Paul be taken into the barracks. He directed that he be flogged and interrogated in order to find out why the people were shouting at him like this. As they stretched him out to flog him, Paul said to the centurion standing there, "Is it legal for you to flog a Roman citizen who hasn't even been found guilty?"

When the centurion heard this, he went to the commander and reported it. "What are you going to do?" he asked. "This man is a Roman citizen." The commander went to Paul and asked, "Tell me, are you a Roman citizen?"

"Yes, I am," he answered. Then the commander said, "I had to pay a lot of money for my citizenship." "But I was born a citizen," Paul replied. Those who were about to interrogate him withdrew immediately. The commander himself was alarmed when he realized that he had put Paul, a Roman citizen, in chains.

Acts 22:22–29 (NIV)

Therefore go and make disciples of all nations, baptizing them in the name of the Father and of the Son and of the Holy Spirit.

Matthew 28:19 (NIV)

ENGAGE

Fascination with Genius

As humans, we are fascinated by genius in all forms. Whether it be the more classical characterisations of genius as embodied by Einstein or Beethoven; or the type of genius expressed by Picasso or even David Beckham, we love to read about such figures and revel in watching or thinking about how they do what they do best. The movie *Good Will Hunting* featured one such genius who, whilst working as a janitor, showed up some of the greatest minds at Harvard University as he solved their challenging mathematical proof with ease.

Multiple Intelligences

Measuring intelligence has also been the subject of study by academics for years. During most of the twentieth century, intelligence quotient (IQ) figured as the definitive measurement of intelligence. But as the twenty-first century dawned, many academics began to explore other aspects of intelligence, not so easily captured by the standard IQ tests. Scholars began to recognise genius in the mastery of one's body, as in the case cited above of David Beckham. They also began to explore the genius behind engaging in interpersonal exchanges. IQ was no longer the de facto measurement of genius. It was now joined by things like emotional quotient (EQ), measuring emotional intelligence.

Cultural Intelligence

Out of this exploration of multiple intelligences, researchers in the business community began to recognise that there were certain business leaders who had developed skills that allowed them to succeed and thrive in the global marketplace. Other leaders, who had thrived when leading their domestic companies, seemed to struggle when it came to engaging with business leaders and situations in other cultures. Two business researchers in particular, Chris Earley at Purdue and his colleague, Soon Ang in Singapore, developed the concept of cultural intelligence (CQ) as a means to describe those qualities that allowed some leaders to flourish in an intercultural environment and how the lack of such qualities created difficulties for others in similar situations. Cultural intelligence is a globally recognised way of assessing and improving effectiveness in cross-cultural situations.

The literary figure who would surely have one of the highest CQ scores for his cultural intelligence is Ian Fleming's international spy, James Bond. When we think of the character of James Bond, it is clear he thrives in interpersonal exchanges played out in cross-cultural settings. He is able to fit into diverse cultural contexts almost seamlessly. Keeping James Bond in mind, the various aspects of cultural intelligence become very clear.

The Cultural Intelligence Centre has found that the culturally intelligent have strengths in four capabilities. That is drive, knowledge, strategy, and action. The first is one's motivation or drive to interact in culturally diverse settings. Looking at the different missions in which James Bond engages, one gets the clear impression that he thrives on intercultural engagement. The audience feels that James Bond would not be content if the scope of his work were confined to the United Kingdom. Without this inner drive, individuals find it difficult to make the effort required to engage in otherwise valuable intercultural exchanges.

The second aspect of cultural intelligence is one's knowledge of cultural customs, norms, and expectations. Whether his mission lands him in

Beijing or Saudi Arabia, James Bond always seems to be prepared with the requisite knowledge of the appropriate cultural behaviours. But what makes the missions compelling is that there is often something unexpected and unaccounted for that crops up to challenge Bond in these intercultural settings. This brings us to the third aspect of cultural intelligence, which is strategy. Strategic thinking involves using one's knowledge to plan ahead and anticipate, but it also encompasses the ability to think on one's feet and adapt to a changing landscape. This characteristic is one of the key features in making James Bond such an enjoyable character to follow. This ability is also tied up in the final aspect of cultural intelligence, which is action. The strategy element is simply the mental planning and the mental shifting of understanding as a situation changes. The action component is the ability to actually behave in a way commensurate with the planning or the unexpected new situation.

The Necessity of Cross-Cultural Interaction for Believers

So what does James Bond, or cultural intelligence in general, have to do with the message of the Gospel? It is true that ministry can take place in a singular cultural environment disconnected from the other cultural contexts; but in an ever globalising society, such situations are now the exception to the rule. Jesus reiterated to his disciples that the greatest commandment God gave was to "love the Lord your God with all your heart and with all your soul and with all your mind" and to "love your neighbour as yourself." There are still some neighbourhoods and areas of the world that are extremely homogenous and do not exhibit much cultural diversity. But for most of us, we do not have to travel to a foreign country to experience cultural diversity; we are surrounded by it. Today, in our city of London and other major metropolitan cities worldwide, the breadth of cultural diversity is staggering. Like other such cities, London has small (and sometimes large) sub-communities of individuals who have brought their culture with them from all corners of the world. London is a case in point where almost all the nationalities, ethnicities, and generational groups are represented. Even within such culturally diverse contexts, ministry does not always require much in terms of cultural intelligence. Jesus's Parable of the Good Samaritan is a prime example: where two individuals from very different cultures interact with each other, and ministry takes place without any overt knowledge of the other's culture. Basic human needs are evident, and the Samaritan meets those needs willingly.

Having said that, our risen Lord left us with instructions that we "go and make disciples of all nations, baptising them in the name of the Father and of the Son and of the Holy Spirit" (Matthew 28:19) and that we should be his "witnesses in Jerusalem, in all Judea and Samaria, and to the ends of the earth" (Acts 1:8). Fulfilling this command of the risen Lord and spreading the Gospel message requires interaction with cultures other than our own. Our increasingly global world community requires it as well. If we are going to interact cross-culturally, as we must, it will be helpful to develop the tools and skills needed for these to be successful interactions. The concept of cultural intelligence gives us a lens through which to understand how well or ill equipped we are for this task and can highlight areas where we might improve the quality of these interactions.

During my many years of ministry, I have come across people or congregations who want to love their neighbours from other cultural backgrounds. They have a strong desire to love, but they do not know how to go about it. Cultural intelligence can be a helpful tool. Culture matters, whether national, ethnical, generational, or organisational. Some people need to *belong* before they *believe*; they want to be *loved* before they are told about the Word. The Word of God can be preached without words! It is conveyed through action and by how well we receive people who are different from us.

Culture also shapes how we read and interpret the Bible. Mark Powell in his book, *How Do They Hear? Bridging the Gap between the Pulpit and Pew*, wrote about an experiment with twelve American theology students who were given the parable of the prodigal son to read and memorise and, later, to share what they had read. On sharing, not one of them referred to the famine in Luke 15:14 as the cause of why the prodigal son was in the pig house: "After he had spent everything, there was a severe famine in that whole country, and he began to be in need." They omitted the famine; what they chose to focus on was influenced by their cultural and social background. With this surprising result, he went on to run another study with a hundred American students of different races, ages, religions, and socioeconomic status. Ninety-four did not mention famine; only six mentioned famine as the cause. For them, the parable meant that the son squandered the money.

When the same experiment was conducted in Russia and Tanzania, both identified different causes as to why he ended up in a pig house. In Petersburg, Russia, Powell did the same experiment with fifty Russians; forty-two mentioned famine as the reason, while only eight did not mention famine. He went on to write that Russian past experience with famine was a great influence in what they chose to notice. The Russians did not say anything about the prodigal son squandering his wealth. In Tanzania, another very different cultural background, when they were asked the same question, many said that the reason why he ended up in the pig house was because no one gave him anything to eat. Tanzania's main cultural background is Ubuntu: "I am because we are." Why this different interpretation? Culture matters greatly when we interpret the Bible. What we choose to notice is determined by our culture.

Globalisation in the Early Church: The Tale of Two Apostles: Peter and Paul

The question of globalisation was one of the most important questions in the early church; it caused a great deal of debate. It is hard to overstate the importance of this debate and the emotional investment that each of the players in the early church had in it. The issue that arose around globalisation was that of circumcision. Was circumcision a religious rite that surrounded inclusion into the Way, the name given to Christianity at this early stage, or was it a cultural rite with religious significance only to adherents of the Jewish faith? At the time, Judaism and Christianity were so intricately entwined that this was no small question, and different leaders in the apostolic community took different positions.

Acts 15 informs us of the existence of this dispute in the city of Antioch and mentions that it really affected Paul and Barnabas. It goes on to state that both proponents came to Jerusalem, where the church elders heard the matter and made a sweeping decree concerning the relationship between the Gentiles and the Law of Moses.

But in Paul's letter to the Galatians, we get to see the question from Paul's perspective and just how upbeat he was. Paul calls the church leaders (James, Peter, and John) names: "those who seemed to be important"(2:6) and "those reputed to be pillars"(2:9). Whereas in Acts 15, Peter would seem to be on the same page as Paul and preaching to Gentiles himself (see his speech in Acts 15:7–11), Paul distinguishes himself from Peter directly, calling Peter an apostle to the Jews (Galatians 2:7–8), and calling himself an apostle to the Gentiles (Galatians 2:7–8). He then openly chastises Peter as a hypocrite, calling into question both his Jewishness and his commitment to the Gospel, because of his behaviour among a mixed Jewish/Gentile congregation. When we look at Paul's letter to the Corinthians, it becomes clear that even the decree from the Apostolic council in Jerusalem did not sit well with Paul. In response to a question in the church about food sacrificed to idols, Paul does not refer the Corinthian Christians to the apostolic document but completely undermines it with his response to them (1 Corinthians 8).

In order to understand how it is that Paul and Peter, two pillars of the early church who both loved Jesus, who were committed to the worldwide spread of the Gospel, and who were both filled with the Holy Spirit, could take such different positions on this issue, it is important to compare their respective backgrounds and, ultimately, their cross-cultural competence. Paul's background was ideal for making him a global leader in the Christian church, at the forefront of cross-cultural communication of Christ's message. Peter's background, along with that of John and James, was much more limiting and prevented him from being able to interact effectively outside the Jewish community.

In terms of languages, Paul spoke Greek fluently, and if this was not his first language, it was certainly the language he used in the majority of his daily interactions. This fluency came from Paul's training in the synagogue, where he studied the Septuagint Greek translation of the Old Testament and also needed to be able to converse with the political authorities in his position as a Pharisee. Paul had a thorough classical Greek education, including rhetoric and philosophy. But because this training took place in the Judean context, it gave him a very clear sense of the boundaries between the two cultures and an awareness of the differences. In terms of motivational factors, as an upper class Judean Pharisee, Paul continually moved in social circles that were diverse. The Judean politicians interacted regularly with the local Roman politicians. He also likely travelled extensively, even prior to his conversion experience, and was travelling when our Lord appeared to him. His friends and colleagues would have encouraged his interacting with multiple individuals from varied cultural backgrounds.

Apart from being widely travelled, Paul was also a Roman citizen; he had dual citizenship, like many of us have today. As someone with dual citizenship myself, I am likely to be more culturally aware of my own culture and the cultures of others than those who have not been out of their locality. Read about Paul's encounter with the Roman soldiers and Jewish people on his return to Jerusalem from his missionary journey.

Read Acts 22:22–29.

Paul was widely travelled; he held dual citizenship and spoke languages other than Aramaic. These factors show why his cross-cultural competence was high. He was set aside for this ministry by God, and one of the ways was to open doors through the factors named above. By placing you in a very diverse setting, God does intend that you engage.

Peter, on the other hand, spoke only Aramaic. He may have had a passing familiarity with Greek, enough to ask a pointed question here or there, but he was certainly not comfortable speaking the language. As a fisherman, Peter had a minimal education. Belonging to the lower economic tier, his social circle would have been very much less diverse in nature. When Peter and Paul are examined through the lens of their respective cultural intelligence, it becomes clear that Paul's life experience gave him a high cross-cultural competence, whereas Peter's life experiences left him woefully lacking in this area. God used these life experience to grow the church in different ways. Peter clearly had a heart for the Gentiles, as his speech in Acts indicates, but he was ill-equipped to act on it with much of an impact. Therefore, his primary ministry remained one to the Jews, as Paul stated. Paul, on the other hand, was well-equipped to spread the message of the Gospel throughout the Roman world, because of his high CQ. Lacking CQ does not prevent us from being used by God, but increasing our CQ will allow us to do so much more.

Peter could stay within the Jewish circles because these were very early days of globalisation, unlike today, where all nations are within a city. In a city like London, almost all the nations and cultures are represented. In my current church, Tooting Junction Baptist, we have over eighteen different nationalities and different races worshipping together, including different age groups, from one to ninety years old, and different socio-economic classes.

Tooting, where I work, is a very diverse community; you can find people from almost every corner of the world. The city of London is even called "the global city" by some people. Many years ago, missionaries left the United Kingdom to preach to the world, but now God has turned the table around: the world has come to the United Kingdom. What do we do about that? How do we engage with what God is doing? Walking along Green Street in East London will remind you of Pakistan, because of the people, businesses, rich culture, and religious symbols, in the area.

There are other cities with homogenous cultures, where we might not require high cross-cultural competence to do mission or ministry work. But when you find yourself in cities like London, Kuala Lumpur, or New York, you certainly will need to improve your cross-cultural competence level for an effective mission and ministry. The good news is that cultural intelligence can be improved after taking an assessment; with the help of a coach, you can improve your cross-cultural competence. We will talk about this later in the book.

Expanding the Intercultural Definition to Include Subcultures and Generational Gaps

The classical definition of CQ, created for a business context, focuses primarily on ethnic cultural differences.

It is not only in the area of ethnicity and nationality that culture matters but also in the area of generational and organisational differences. I currently serve in a church with a multigenerational congregation, with some members in their nineties, fifties, twenties, teens, and children. We have intentionally created an enabling environment for worship, ministry, discipleship, and mission with the goal of carrying everybody along. Though it was not easy at the beginning, we are now enjoying the fruits of a multigenerational fellowship. We have organised two very big festivals at our local Common, Figges Marsh, and every year we run a barbecue for the community. All the different generational groups participate in the planning and execution of the festivals and the barbecue.

Returning to the apostolic figurehead Paul, we can see that he was very good at working across generations. In the letter to Timothy, we read about how Paul spent time mentoring Timothy. On occasion, he tells Timothy not to allow people to look down on him because he is young. How did Paul know that this would be the case with Timothy? He knew also that Timothy could easily be distracted as a youth. Paul's level of cross-cultural competence certainly extended to subcultures other than ethnicity and nationality. He knew how to relate well to young people. In his letter to Timothy, he wrote:

> "Don't let anyone look down on you because you are young, but set an example for the believers in speech, in conduct, in love, in faith and in purity. Until I come, devote yourself to the public reading of Scripture, to preaching and to teaching. Do not neglect your gift,

which was given you through prophecy when the body
of elders laid their hands on you." 1 Timothy 4:12–14

Subcultural differences like age, organisation, and gender can be just
as divisive and require just as much work and acumen to transcend as
cultural differences. In this context, the ability to interact with different
subcultures and generations requires understanding and increased
cultural intelligence.

Apart from that, there is also the organisational culture. Different
denominations have different cultures. In my ministry, I have seen a
lot of cultural differences when Pentecostals worship with Anglicans or
Baptists. The Pentecostal might see the Baptist as not being truly active
in worship, since they do not completely free themselves during worship.
The Baptist, on the other hand, might see the Pentecostal as being
shallow in content. They may come from different ethnic or national
backgrounds, but over time, the organisations or denominations shape
the way they worship and share fellowship.

APPLY

Questions for Group Discussion

1) Can you think of a time in your life when you saw cultural
   intelligence at work (either on your part or someone else who
   was with you in the situation)? Would you feel comfortable
   sharing the story with the group?

2) Do you identify more with Peter, in terms of a more sheltered
   set of life experiences, or do you identify more with Paul, feeling
   that your life experiences have prepared you for very successful
   intercultural interactions?

3) If you have children, do you think you are preparing them more
   as a Peter or as a Paul?

4) Can you think of any situations in your life where cultural intelligence would have helped, but you lacked the cultural knowhow that would have improved the situation?

5) What aspects of your life do you think would benefit by improving your cultural intelligence?

6) How could you make cultural intelligence a part of your lifestyle?

RESULTS

Scripture warns us not only to be hearers of the Word but also to be doers of the Word. Reflect on what you have studied in this chapter and consider sharing together when the group comes together next time.

PART 1

Cultural Intelligence Drive in Cross-Cultural Ministry, Mission and the Workplace

Cultural intelligence drive. This is your level of interest, drive, and motivation to adapt to intercultural missions and ministries.

The cultural intelligence drive consists of intrinsic drive, extrinsic drive, and self-confidence.

Chapter 2

Intrinsic Motivation in Cross-Cultural Church and Ministry

PREPARE

Jonah Flees From the LORD

The word of the Lord came to Jonah son of Amittai: "Go to the great city of Nineveh and preach against it, because its wickedness has come up before me." But Jonah ran away from the Lord and headed for Tarshish. He went down to Joppa, where he found a ship bound for that port. After paying the fare, he went aboard and sailed for Tarshish to flee from the Lord.

Then the Lord sent a great wind on the sea, and such a violent storm arose that the ship threatened to break up. All the sailors were afraid and each cried out to his own god. And they threw the cargo into the sea to lighten the ship. But Jonah had gone below deck, where he lay down and fell into a deep sleep. The captain went to him and said, "How can you sleep? Get up and call on your god! Maybe he will take notice of us so that we will not perish."

Then the sailors said to each other, "Come, let us cast lots to find out who is responsible for this calamity." They cast lots and the lot fell on Jonah. So they asked him, "Tell us, who is responsible for making all this trouble for us? What kind of work do you do? Where do you come from? What is your country? From what people are you?" He answered, "I am a Hebrew and I worship the Lord, the God of heaven, who made the sea and the dry land."

This terrified them and they asked, "What have you done?" (They knew he was running away from the Lord, because he had already told them so.)

The sea was getting rougher and rougher. So they asked him, "What should we do to you to make the sea calm down for us?" "Pick me up and throw me into the sea," he replied, "and it will become calm. I know that it is my fault that this great storm has come upon you."

Instead, the men did their best to row back to land. But they could not, for the sea grew even wilder than before. Then they cried out to the Lord, "Please, Lord, do not let us die for taking this man's life. Do not hold us accountable for killing an innocent man, for you, Lord, have done as you pleased." Then they took Jonah and threw him overboard, and the raging sea grew calm. At this the men greatly feared the Lord, and they offered a sacrifice to the Lord and made vows to him.

Now the Lord provided a huge fish to swallow Jonah, and Jonah was in the belly of the fish three days and three nights.

Jonah 1: 1-17 (NIV)

ENGAGE

The Dual Nature of Intrinsic Motivation

The cultural intelligence scale was created with the business world in mind. If you are operating a multinational business and want to select the best candidate to head up negotiations and interactions with foreign subsidiaries and other business interests, what qualities should you be looking for in your ideal candidate? One of the key components that researchers found characterised successful multinational business leaders was a strong intrinsic motivation related to diverse and new intercultural experiences. Part of this relates to simple personality types and traits, and another part relates to deep-seated personal values and beliefs.

In missions and ministries, there are some individuals who simply find new settings and cultural experiences to be an energising force in their life. They thrive on such experiences and can't wait until the next one. Other individuals are quite terrified by such new and different experiences and find them quite taxing. I have always loved working cross-culturally, right from my days as an entrepreneur. This has followed me into ministry. When I came to England, the first church I attended was a Baptist church, with all members being from one particular African country. I felt something was missing. I wanted to engage with other cultures, especially the locals, as I saw myself as a missionary to England. Within a very short time, I relocated to another church with majority locals, and I saw my effectiveness increase in service. I also have a friend who is terrified of working across cultures; there is always this feeling that he will be misunderstood and devalued. This difference in attitude and response to these experiences correlates highly to differences in the extroversion versus introversion scale in personality types. While it is possible to push oneself and engage in such activities despite negative emotions or the like, these personality traits are tied up with our individual character and seem to be coded into the very fabric of our DNA. This is one aspect of cultural intelligence that seems to be pretty well set and not something that can be cultivated—you either have it or you don't, and it is good to know either way. However, research in behavioural and social psychology is increasingly showing that most people are actually ambiverts. They fall somewhere between these extremes (see this news article from the *Wall Street Journal*: http://www.wsj.com/articles/not-an-introvert-not-an-extrovert-you-may-be-an-ambivert-1438013534).

But beyond the sense of inherent excitement that comes along with such experiences, individuals assign different values to varying activities and experiences, based on their personality and worldview. What we value and find important can be just as motivating as what we find enjoyable and exciting. Moreover, our sense of values changes over time and can be influenced by various factors. So, whereas the inherent enjoyment that we derive from certain activities tends to be a fixed part of our personality, the value we place on an activity is more fluid. If we decide that we want to change our level of internal motivation for intercultural activities, the best way to do so is by increasing the value we find in such activities. Someone with an extroverted personality might enjoy meeting and making new friends, but if they do not value people from cultures different from theirs, their motivation to engage with the "other" will be very low (unless they increase the value they have for the other).

Contemporary Example: Short-Term Mission Trip

Think about what happens when a church youth group plans to take a short-term mission trip. David Livermore writes extensively about such short-term mission trips and the implications that the cultural intelligence construct has on them. Imagine it is 2010 and news of the devastation wrought by the earthquake in Haiti has aroused a great deal of media attention. The youth group of the church has about twelve high school students who attend regularly enough to consider going on the trip. The youth pastor has talked with each of the students individually and has noticed four different categories into which the students fall.

	Looks Forward to a Foreign Trip	Dreads a Foreign Trip
Values Missionary Work	Enthusiastic Volunteers	Reluctant Volunteers
Missions Work Is 'Selfish'	Cynical Volunteers	Uninterested Nonparticipants

This chart treats these as extreme options, but obviously, a grid showing varying levels within these categories would be even more accurate. The point in this example is that internal motivation has at least two components; one relates to your values and priorities, while the other relates to what you enjoy and what interests you.

But here again, there are many components to an intercultural experience. One individual may find tasting exotic foods more enjoyable, whereas another may find dealing with a foreign language more enjoyable. Similarly, there are different aspects to an intercultural experience that one might place value on. If you can learn to identify those aspects of intercultural interactions that excite and motivate you and other aspects that might deter you from such interactions, you are then in a better position to identify the types of intercultural experiences that might appeal most to you.

18

Biblical Example: Jonah and Nineveh

Consider the case of Jonah. In the story of this Hebrew prophet, we can see the negative impact that the lack of internal motivation can have. Jonah receives the word of the Lord to go and prophesy to Nineveh. But rather than obeying the Lord, he hitches a ride aboard a ship and hightails it in the opposite direction; hardly the behaviour of an obedient prophet of the Lord. After God rebukes him for his disobedience by using the natural elements, Jonah finally relents and obeys his original directive. After he is successful in his mission, he then sulks like a child, and we learn specifically why Jonah did not want to obey the original command that he received. The fourth chapter of the book of Jonah has the following statement:

> "But Jonah was greatly displeased and became angry. He prayed to the LORD, "O LORD, is this not what I said when I was still at home? That is why I was so quick to flee to Tarshish. I knew that you are a gracious and compassionate God, slow to anger and abounding in love, a God who relents from sending calamity. Now, O LORD, take away my life, for it is better for me to die than to live."

In this prayer, Jonah makes it clear that his value system did not allow for the redemption of the city of Nineveh. He could not forgive the city for the evil that he saw there and, therefore, had no internal motivation to follow the external command that he received from the Lord to go there and preach. Although the story does not explicitly mention Jonah's past history with Nineveh and why he might so utterly despise the people there, it is likely that he did not have any warm feelings about interacting with its culture. There are not many instances of a Hebrew prophet actually being sent to a foreign city or country to prophesy. Virtually all of the prophets' messages were directed either to the people of Israel or the people of Judah. Even the prophecies against other nations (like those of Isaiah, directed against Assyria, Babylon, Egypt, Moab, and Edom) appear to have been delivered in Judah and not in the land against whom the oracle was directed. Therefore, Jonah's status as a prophet does not indicate whether he interacted easily with other cultures or not. But as the story reads, it seems clear that he did not interact easily with the Assyrian city of Nineveh.

In either case, the Lord does not rebuke Jonah because of his culturally confined personality. It is because his heart is not right that he becomes the object of the Lord's rebuke. His values are out of sync with those of the Lord, which prevents him from carrying out the Lord's will. But in this case, we see that he is still able to complete the command without aligning his values with the Lord's. Internal motivation is necessary for a high CQ and for a successful career involving intercultural dynamics, but the lack of internal motivation to make such interactions happen does not mean that they will not happen.

CASE STUDY

Iyabo and Tony are a Nigerian couple who received an immigrant visa that enabled them to work and live in the United Kingdom. In Nigeria, Iyabo was doing very well in her career as a banker, and she was also a teacher in her church Sunday School. On arrival, they decided to look for a church to attend. They visited the Redeemed Christian Church of God close to their house. Iyabo enjoyed the service. "This is just like my church in Nigeria. I love it here! I would like to come back to this church," she said. Tony insisted that they try other churches, as he wanted something different from what he was already used to. The next Sunday, they went to a Church of England service, with a very diverse congregation; the service was very slow and quiet. Tony enjoyed the service and wanted to come back. All members were invited to wait for refreshments after the service. Tony and Iyabo went into the hall for refreshments. Iyabo felt very uncomfortable with people who were very different from her and said she would not go back to the church. She found it very boring and felt that this was not a church she could attend. After much argument, they decided to attend two different churches in a single Sunday.

After three years in London, Tony had only changed jobs once, advancing from a smaller retail shop to a bigger retail shop. He loved his work very much and always looked forward to it. On the other hand, Iyabo was having problems keeping a job. She had changed her job over eight times, moving from one career path to another, always complaining that her colleagues did not like her. She thought another academic certificate would provide her with more success in her workplace, but it did not change anything. Iyabo is not happy in London. Iyabo met a friend who asked her a very important question: "How do you feel inside when you meet people who are different from you? Which cultures do you have the hardest time relating with?" As she tried to answer these questions, Iyabo realised that she hated interacting with cultures that were different from her own.

Improving Your Intrinsic CQ Drive for Cross-Cultural Church and Ministry

David Livermore suggests that one major way to improve the Intrinsic Interest aspect of your CQ is by connecting an existing interest with an intercultural component. Paul was a very zealous Pharisee, very passionate about what he believed as a Pharisee; when his belief changed, he connected that same zealousness to his new cultural environment, which was very different from the former. My own experience was similar. I studied business and have always loved business planning and strategising. I spent many years running a business in Nigeria. When I moved to the United Kingdom to study theology, which allowed me to become a pastor, I was able to reconnect my interest and love for entrepreneurship with my ministry in a very diverse cultural setting. Serving as chair of the Mission Strategy Forum of the London Baptist Association has always been a very rewarding ministry for me.

One popular avenue that some take in order to connect an existing interest with an intercultural component is in the area of sports. Sports fans in one particular culture can easily transfer their enthusiasm for the sport from their own home team to a local team from another culture. Pets provide another great way to cross-cultural boundaries. Here in the

United Kingdom, if you love pets, meeting people from other cultures who share that love of pets too can quickly open doors for conversation and friendship. Identifying your current interests may provide you with an enjoyable means to engage with another culture.

APPLY

Discussion Questions

1) What are the types of activities for which you know you have a high internal motivation? Describe how you feel when you engage in those activities.

2) What are the types of activities for which you know you have a very low internal motivation? Describe how you feel when you engage in those activities.

3) Are there certain intercultural events/activities/situations that seem to align more closely for you than others?

4) In your workplace, how would you rate your intrinsic motivation to engage in intercultural interactions with customers/clients/students/co-workers/colleagues?

5) In your personal family situation, how would you rate your intrinsic motivation to engage in intercultural interactions with spouse/in-laws/parents/grandparents?

6) What types of values are you fostering (or do you hope to foster) in your children concerning intercultural interactions?

7) In the above case study, why do you think Iyabo can't keep her job or enjoy cross-cultural interactions?

8) How do you feel inside when you meet people who are different from you?

9) If you were in Iyabo's position, what would you do to make sure that you got along well with people from other cultures?

10) If you were in Jonah's position, what would you have done differently?

11) Are there ways we might behave like Jonah in the church today? Please list.

RESULTS

Scripture warns us not only to be hearers of the Word but also to be doers of the Word. As you spend time living out some of the principles learnt in this chapter, write out below a reflection on how you apply them to practical issues. When the group comes together next time, consider sharing with each other your experiences

Chapter 3

External (Extrinsic) Motivation in Cross-Cultural Church and Ministry

PREPARE

David among the Philistines

But David thought to himself, "One of these days I will be destroyed by the hand of Saul. The best thing I can do is to escape to the land of the Philistines. Then Saul will give up searching for me anywhere in Israel, and I will slip out of his hand."

So David and the six hundred men with him left and went over to Achish son of Maok king of Gath. David and his men settled in Gath with Achish. Each man had his family with him, and David had his two wives: Ahinoam of Jezreel and Abigail of Carmel, the widow of Nabal. When Saul was told that David had fled to Gath, he no longer searched for him.

Then David said to Achish, "If I have found favour in your eyes, let a place be assigned to me in one of the country towns, that I may live there. Why should your servant live in the royal city with you?"

So on that day Achish gave him Ziklag, and it has belonged to the kings of Judah ever since. David lived in Philistine territory a year and four months.

Now David and his men went up and raided the Geshurites, the Girzites and the Amalekites. (From ancient times these peoples had lived in the land extending to Shur and Egypt.) Whenever David attacked an area, he did not leave a man or woman alive, but took sheep and cattle, donkeys and camels, and clothes. Then he returned to Achish.

When Achish asked, "Where did you go raiding today?" David would say, "Against the Negev of Judah" or "Against the Negev of Jerahmeel" or "Against the Negev of the Kenites." He did not leave a man or woman alive to be brought to Gath, for he thought, "They might inform on us and say, 'This is what David did.'" And such was his practice as long as he lived in Philistine territory. Achish trusted David and said to himself, "He has become so obnoxious to his people, the Israelites, that he will be my servant for life."

1 Samuel 27:1-12(NIV)

Further Reading

1 Samuel 28 and 29

ENGAGE

Introduction

Think for a moment about what motivates the character James Bond to engage in those outrageous assignments that involve state dinners at royal palaces or exclusive underground nightclubs at the far reaches of the globe. Bond certainly had the intrinsic motivation for these types of venues. The audience gets the impression that he is enjoying himself the most when he is socially engaging with individuals from completely different cultures. But with Bond, you see more than just internal motivating factors. It is very clear that there are multiple external factors that provide ample motivation for Bond's rendezvous with the world's cultures. In his capacity as a secret agent for the government, his jurisdiction is primarily focused on foreign threats to the nation. Therefore, foreign diplomacy is a prime component of his job. Stopping someone from destroying the country is a pretty strong external motivator. There are also the social perks. Inevitably, such situations require him to interact closely with beautiful women. In considering the motivating factors that lead us to engage in intercultural situations, external motivation is an essential element of the motivational process.

Defining External Motivation vis-à-vis Internal Motivation

One's intrinsic/internal motivation is the motivational power of the behaviour/interaction in and of itself. It involves the joy one feels while engaging in the behaviour as well as the satisfaction that one derives from having been involved in the interaction. External motivation does not focus on the interaction directly but rather on the benefits that follow from engaging in such an interaction. External motivations are more fluid than internal motivations and not as directly tied to the behaviour itself. It may happen that there are three opportunities for intercultural interaction available to you, where one of them has external motivating factors for you and the other two do not. This will likely be a big factor in terms of what opportunity you choose.

External Motivation in the Life of King David

Writing about the Israelite King David, the anonymous author of the books of Samuel describes a very curious episode in David's life. The current king, Saul, had invited David into the palace, where he became a central part of the political scene and was in close contact with Saul. But the two had a falling out; for years, Saul wanted to kill David, and the narrator provides many instances where Saul tried to. This put David on the run, and when the person trying to kill you is the king, it is difficult to go anywhere in the country where someone will not betray you. David, along with his troops, therefore, retreated to enemy territory. The Philistines were constantly at war with the Israelites throughout the period of the Judges and throughout Saul's reign (1 Samuel 14:52).

But David not only hid among the Philistines, he became so friendly with Achish, the king of Gath (one of the five main cities of the Philistines), that the king gave an entire city to David (1 Samuel 27:5–7).

David lived among the Philistines for more than a year and engaged in military campaigns on behalf of King Achish (1 Samuel 27:8–12). In any case, there is no doubt that David did not foster a relationship with the Philistine king simply out of some intrinsic motivation. David was in fear for his life, and the whole "the enemy of my enemy" line of reasoning applied. David wanted security and a safety net from Saul, who wanted him dead. This external motivation to save his life was enough drive for him to engage with the other. External motivation can be a strong influence for engaging cross-culturally.

Unlike any of the other leaders of Israel, David understood Philistine culture intimately. He had lived among the people, spoken their language (the Philistine language is more like a dialect of Hebrew, and the two are mutually intelligible), eaten their food, and worn their clothes. He knew what the Philistines wanted and how they thought, and he was even privy to some of their military strategy (1 Samuel 28–29). It should come as no surprise then that it was David more than any other Judean king who was able to unite the kingdom (Israel and Judah) and to establish a kingdom with sovereign borders. His son Solomon, himself quite adept at international relations, was the only other Judean king who was able to accomplish this level of peace and unification. Much of David's political success can be attributed to his high CQ. This is also one reason why God, "seeing the heart," chose David as the ruler of the kingdom rather than Saul.

Risks and Rewards of External Motivation with Case Study

External motivation is not a bad thing. On the contrary, it is quite necessary in motivating us to act. As we raise children, we constantly turn to our knowledge and intuitive understanding of external motivation. We make sure that we point out, or even artificially introduce, external motivations to encourage our children to do things they may not otherwise do. Take the case of the Ade family. Their thirteen-year-old daughter, Tosin, was having difficulty with a French class at school. Tosin informed her parents Mr and Mrs Ade of her desire to drop the class; the school's newly implemented rules allowed her to do so. The

Ades both value cultural awareness and want Tosin to succeed, both in school and in her future career, and believe they are in a position to guide her through this decision process. They both immediately recognise that Tosin does not place any value on the experience itself (there is no intrinsic personal motivation present for her to take the class). But because they believe a foreign language is important for her worldview in general, they try to drum up as many external perks as they could possibly conjure. Variations of this exchange take place in households all over the world, on topics ranging from taking a French class to eating your peas!

Parents do not engage in this type of behavioural bullying from some mean-spirited kind of position that they do not want their children to have any fun or enjoy themselves. Nor do they generally think that their children will never derive any joy from the activities they currently don't like (French class or eating peas). In fact, in these situations, most parents believe that if they can get their children to focus on a few external motivating factors in the short term, over time, the behaviour will become enjoyable and valued (thus intrinsically motivated) in the long term. Researchers have studied this interaction between intrinsic and extrinsic motivating factors for an individual's behaviour and have highlighted the circumstances where this natural belief holds true, contrasting them with other circumstances where such well-intentioned encouragement has the opposite effect.

Two researchers in the psychology department at the University of Rochester (Ryan and Deci) have been studying human motivation and self-determination for several decades now, and the question of intrinsic versus extrinsic (what we are calling external) motivation is a primary focus of their research. They agree that intrinsic motivation is a clear and real element of human behavioural motivation and drives our propensity to learn and assimilate new information constantly. But as they have studied external motivating factors, they have found that these factors vary widely in how essential they are to a particular behaviour or situation.

To return to an earlier example, both Mr and Mrs Ade pull Tosin aside at different times to try to convince her of the value of taking French. Mr Ade reminds Tosin of the importance of French in her stated career objective as a fashion designer. He links Tosin's interest in fashion design to the study of French. When most people think of fashion, they think of France. In his conversation with Tosin, Mr Ade highlights a benefit of French class that is essential to Tosin's interest; this is an example of what Ryan and Dice (2008, 182) call an "autonomous motivation" that helps to foster internal motivation. Mrs Ade, on the other hand, remembers that Kola, a romantic interest of Tosin, is also taking French. She tries focusing on that side benefit as a possible motivation for Tosin to continue in the class. The presence of her love interest lies further outside of the content of the class itself and would be an example of a controlled motivation that actually serves to undermine any internal motivation that might have already existed in Tosin (Ryan and Deci, 2008, 182). Even such things that we might think of as more noble motivations, like competitions or rewarding good grades with gifts, fall into this controlled motivation category. Both elements may well be factors in Tosin's decision to keep or drop the class, but it is clear that one is much more important than the other.

An Example with Mission Field

Many years ago, I was appointed mission director of New Covenant Baptist Church in Port Harcourt. Shortly after the appointment, I attended a mission conference organised by the Global Mission Board and International Mission Board at Ede in Nigeria. During the conference, we listened to stories of people in faraway, remote places, where everyday life was very challenging. These people left their comfort zones to serve others in very poor areas. One shared of how his grandfather and father had served in the place he was now serving. These stories completely changed my motivation and increased my drive to engage in cross-cultural missions and ministries. It was this drive, coupled with a lot of other factors, that motivated us as a church to begin a mission field in far-off Burkina Faso, a field that now runs a primary school with over two hundred students and a secondary school with other satellite mission fields all over the country.

Though there was already an intrinsic interest to go out in mission to serve others and point them to Jesus Christ, connecting this great commission interest to the stories shared by these missionaries in the mission field shifted the church's internal focus to engage in mission work. Within a very short space of time, the church planted over twenty churches in Nigeria, Ghana, and Burkina Faso.

Improving Your External Cultural Intelligence Drive

As Christians we do not engage in missions and ministries for our own benefit; we engage because, the benefits to others is very importance to us (Kingdom benefits)

Reflect on Jesus' teaching in Luke 15: 3-7.

"Then Jesus told them this parable, 'Suppose one of you has a hundred sheep and loses one of them. Doesn't he leave the ninety-nine in the open country and go after the lost sheep until he finds it? And when he finds it, he joyfully puts it on his shoulders and goes home. Then he calls his friends and neighbors together and says, 'Rejoice with me; I have found my lost sheep.' I tell you that in the same way there will be more rejoicing in heaven over one sinner who repents than over ninety-nine righteous persons who do not need to repent.'"

The fact that there is great rejoicing in heaven and here on earth, when a soul repents is enough motivation for cross-cultural mission and evangelism.

Apart from the above, we are not alone; the Holy Spirit is with us as we engage cross-culturally in mission and ministry. Jesus said in Matthew 28: 19-20.

"Therefore go and make disciples of all nations, baptizing them in the name of the Father and of the Son and of the Holy Spirit, and teaching them to obey everything I have commanded you. And surely I am with you always, to the very end of the age."

The Holy Spirit works alongside us in all mission and ministry interactions. In view of the fact that some cross-cultural interactions are very challenging, it is always helpful to reward yourself for every successful cross-cultural interactions by giving thanks to God for both small and big things.

Finally spend time in prayers after every difficult cross-cultural interaction to recharge your batteries for more future interactions. We engage in Cross-cultural missions and ministries because we want to please God. "For God so love the world that he gave one and his only Son, that whoever believes in him shall not perish but have eternal life". John 3:16

APPLY

Discussion Questions

1) What have been some external motivating factors that have led you to interact in an intercultural situation that you might otherwise have avoided?

2) In your church, what do you think the leaders would need to put in place to motivate others to engage in the Great Commission, as instructed by Jesus Christ?

3) Please list specific external motivations that you believe will help your engagement with your community.

4) If you were faced with challenges like David, would you run for safety to a community who might not welcome you?

5) What would you do to make sure you get along well within the community?

6) Do you have any external motivation systems established at your church or workplace to encourage intercultural interactions? Should there be any?

7) What steps would you take to motivate your youths to go through all the stages of discipleship classes (if you have a discipleship resource that is in levels)?

RESULTS

Scripture warns us not only to be hearers of the Word but to be doers of the Word. As you spend time living out some of the principles learnt in this chapter, write out below a reflection on how you apply them to practical issues. When next the group comes together, consider sharing with each other your experiences.

Chapter 4

Competence and Confidence in Cross-Cultural Church and Ministry

PREPARE

Signs for Moses

Moses answered, "What if they do not believe me or listen to me and say, 'The Lord did not appear to you'?" Then the Lord said to him, "What is that in your hand?" "A staff," he replied. The Lord said, "Throw it on the ground."

Moses threw it on the ground and it became a snake and he ran from it. Then the Lord said to him, "Reach out your hand and take it by the tail." So Moses reached out and took hold of the snake and it turned back into a staff in his hand. "This," said the Lord, "is so that they may believe that the Lord, the God of their fathers—the God of Abraham, the God of Isaac and the God of Jacob—has appeared to you."

Then the Lord said, "Put your hand inside your cloak." So Moses put his hand into his cloak, and when he took it out, the skin was leprous—it had become as white as snow. "Now put it back into your cloak," he said. So Moses put his hand back into his cloak, and when he took it out, it was restored, like the rest of his flesh.

Then the Lord said, "If they do not believe you or pay attention to the first sign, they may believe the second. But if they do not believe these two signs or listen to you, take some water from the Nile and pour it on the dry ground. The water you take from the river will become blood on the ground." Moses said to the Lord, "Pardon your servant, Lord. I have never been eloquent, neither in the past nor since you have spoken to your servant. I am slow of speech and tongue."

The Lord said to him, "Who gave human beings their mouths? Who makes them deaf or mute? Who gives them sight or makes them blind? Is it not I, the Lord? Now go; I will help you speak and will teach you what to say." But Moses said, "Pardon your servant, Lord. Please send someone else." Then the Lord's anger burned against Moses and he said, "What about your brother, Aaron the Levite? I know he can speak well. He is already on his way to meet you, and he will be glad to see you. You shall speak to him and put words in his mouth; I will help both of you speak and will teach you what to do. He will speak to the people for you, and it will be as if he were your mouth and as if you were God to him. But take this staff in your hand so you can perform the signs with it."

Exodus 4:1–17 NIV

ENGAGE

Introduction

In considering in detail the specific aspects of CQ drive or motivation, we have already touched on the roles that intrinsic and extrinsic motivation play in getting us to engage in cross-cultural experiences and events. The final element in this area of drive and motivation is what the researchers call self-efficacy. More plainly put, this is the confidence that people feel regarding their own ability to engage naturally and competently in a cross-cultural setting. If they believe, rightly or wrongly, that they will embarrass themselves or others in a cross-cultural setting, it is going to be very difficult to convince them to join an activity in such a setting. This forms what might be called a catch-22 situation and probably calls for promoting CQ in our children at a young age.

Like the other factors of CQ drive, self-confidence is a psychological state (or trait) that applies equally to all of the different activities in our lives; we are simply focusing on the cross-cultural element of those activities. We tend to enjoy activities at which we excel in some way. Because of our enjoyment, we engage in these activities more often. As a result, we become more comfortable with them and develop a certain competence surrounding those activities that cause us to excel and to derive further enjoyment. Conversely, we tend to avoid activities at which we do not excel. The less we engage in them, the less competence we have in the particular activity. This lessened competence lowers our interest in the activity further, continuing the downward spiral.

Moses and Pharaoh

The book of Exodus contains a perfect example of this type of lack of confidence and the corresponding refusal to engage in the behaviour. The Israelites are languishing in Egyptian slavery. The Lord wants to release his people from captivity and bring them to the land he promised Abraham, their forefather. The Lord looks around the Israelites and chooses Moses to lead them out of Egypt. But when God himself appears to Moses and informs him of his choice, Moses comes up with every excuse in the book! His first is that no one will believe that he really spoke to God—they will think I am crazy (Exodus 4:1). The Lord silences this objection by giving Moses three miraculous signs (the staff-to-serpent, leprous hand, and water to blood) that he can perform for any skeptic (Exodus 4:2–9). It is then that Moses is forced to address the real root of his anxiety and reticence to perform what the Lord is asking of him. He confesses that he has a speech deficit of some kind (Exodus 4:10). Various interpreters have suggested different meanings for this "slow of speech and tongue" phrase that Moses uses— did Moses stutter? Was he of limited intelligence and vocabulary? It may simply be that he did not speak Egyptian language well. The Lord made clear that he was to speak first to the elders of Israel (Exodus 3:16–17) and then to Pharaoh himself (Exodus 3:18–22). The first objection was clearly directed towards his conversation with the elders, so this second objection may be directed more specifically at his conversation with

Pharaoh. Moses has to think about how to say what he wants to say in Egyptian (a common phenomenon among second language learners), and this causes his Egyptian speech to be very slow and tedious (hardly conducive to smooth intercultural negotiations). God dismisses this outright, reminding Moses who it is that decides whether a man can talk or hear, affirming that he can coach Moses along in the process (Exodus 4:11–12).

This type of humble exchange with the Creator is a very typical element in these narratives where God chooses a prophet (see Isaiah 6:5; Jeremiah 1:6). But what is not typical here is that Moses does not allow the Lord to lessen his doubts, fears, and objections but persists with them, pleading for the Lord to send someone else, despite the fact that it will infuriate him (Exodus 4:13). Infuriate him it does, but he conforms to Moses' objections and allows Aaron, Moses' brother, to be Moses' mouthpiece to Pharaoh (Exodus 4:14–16). It would seem that Aaron had paid more attention in Egyptian class and used his Egyptian on a more regular basis than did Moses! This episode serves to demonstrate just how debilitating and paralysing low self-confidence can be regarding specific tasks.

Relationship between Competence and Confidence

One should bear in mind that competence in an area is not the same as confidence; the two do not necessarily go hand in hand. When these two are out of sync, it can be disastrous. The starkest picture of this would be in most of the characters played by Jim Carrey early in his career. In his *Ace Ventura* movies, he played the bumbling idiot who would proceed to make a fool out of himself but was blissfully unaware that he was doing so. Not only was the character unaware of how off-putting his behaviour appeared, but he had a grossly misplaced amount of self-confidence in his own competence in social situations. Jim Carrey portrayed many variations on this same character in his early movies; it is what put him on the map as an actor.

But the opposite imbalance is also a tragedy; for example, having the ability but no confidence. The early American poet Emily Dickinson was quite secretive about her writing and had asked her sister to burn her work after her death. Although she clearly enjoyed writing and was more than competent at the task, several experiences in her life had made her reclusive and lacking the self-confidence to share her talents with the world.

As opposed to either of these imbalanced states, it is important for our development in cultural intelligence, along with every other aspect of our life, to grow in confidence as we grow in competence. The two should slide together, as when increasing the size of a picture on your computer with a fixed ratio. As you increase the height, the width increases proportionately. This same logic should hold for our competence and confidence in interacting with people from other cultures. As we gain experience and insight into the cultural dynamics that shape the worlds of our friends and learn to use this knowledge to interact with them, we should begin to feel more comfortable in such foreign environments, which in turn should make us more confident about participating in further similar activities.

Minority Churches: Competence and Confidence

I have served as a church leader in the United Kingdom for many years, serving in multicultural congregations very different from my own culture. In this role, I have met many gifted pastors who are very competent in what they do in missions and ministries. But I have noticed a lack of confidence when it comes to cross-cultural missions, which seems to stem from their awareness of their own accent and inability to speak English well. I remember working with a BME pastor who was doing very well with a church with a monoethnic make-up. While he possessed every gift imaginable to successfully lead a multicultural church, the confidence to engage in an intercultural setting was not there. Although he had the intrinsic and extrinsic interest to engage in such a setting, he did not have the confidence to do it. Why? Because of the judgements he was afraid that people would make when they heard him speak. He explained to me how people from other cultures were always asking him to repeat what he said when he talked with them. Apart from being self-conscious about his heavy accent, he also believed that his English was not good enough. This lack of confidence kept him confined to working in a monoethnic church.

In my case, when I came to the United Kingdom, I joined a cross-cultural church, where I was asked to preach. I am not sure that my competence was high, but I certainly had the confidence to engage, to speak, and to lead. Over the years, my competence has gradually increased. Lack of confidence can stifle spiritual gifts in leaders, especially those who are interested in cross-cultural missions and ministry. It is possible that my eighteen years as an entrepreneur and employer in the business world may have given me the confidence I needed to engage in ministry and missions in cross-cultural settings. If you do not have past experiences to boost your confidence, like in my case, taking a cultural intelligence assessment and attending a workshop will be very helpful. Apart from that, you could also work closely with people from other cultures. In my past ministries, I worked very closely with two ladies from other cultures. I learnt quite a lot from them, and they were very supportive to my ministry.

Male Hubris versus Female Humility

Since competence and confidence run along two completely different axis and do not necessarily move in tandem as they should, it is interesting that there are both gender and cultural patterns that emerge when researchers study attitudes versus ability. In 1999, three research psychologists teamed up to test how individuals perceived their own intelligence and how they perceived that of their siblings and parents. The psychologist based in Tennessee tested the American population, the psychologist based in London tested the British population, and the psychologist based in Moroika tested the Japanese population. Their joint study (published in 2001) revealed some fascinating results.

In terms of gender biases, the men in all three countries clearly had such a bias, while the women in all three countries did not. This bias was apparent when the male participants estimated their own IQ and that of their fathers higher than they estimated those of their sisters and mothers. But like many biases, this one resides in the subconscious, hidden from recognition by these males, or it is a source of embarrassment for them that they are not willing to admit. This stems from the fact that only a small percentage of the male participants acknowledged a belief that males were more intelligent than females in general. Interestingly, this bias disappeared when the male participants focused on emotional intelligence instead of IQ.

So why does this matter, anyway? What this should tell us is that our beliefs about our own competence in various tasks, our self-confidence, is not formed or shaped in a bubble. Instead, it is nurtured in a particular environment. Whether we focus on the male culture in contrast to the female culture, or the British culture in contrast to the Japanese culture, these cultural settings can impact our self-confidence.

Cultural Competence Predicts Creativity: Case Study with Movie Characters and Missionaries

In the film *Selma,* David Oyelowo played the role of Dr. Martin Luther King, Jr. in his fight for blacks to have the freedom to vote in America. When I interviewed David before the release of the film in the United Kingdom, I asked him how it was that a Nigerian British, who spent most of his time in the United Kingdom and Nigeria and grew up with Nigerian parents, was able to play the role of Dr. King so well. His reply to my question was quite telling. He described how Nigerian society approaches child-rearing in a different way than the West. His parents and the wider Nigerian society as a whole raised him with such a positive self-esteem that he could think of himself as a king, even in the humblest of circumstances. This upbringing gave him the confidence he needed to play characters from cultural backgrounds quite different from his own.

He also spoke about how his subsequent British education gave him the competence and depth necessary to be creative and finally how his living in the United States had positively enhanced his entrepreneurial skills in the film industry. This highlights the way in which David's confidence and competence was shaped in large part by his particular environment. David strongly believed that this role was set aside for him by God, who used many people to fulfil that purpose. Another film that is quite fascinating in terms of cross cultures is *Concussions*, where Will Smith plays the role of a Nigerian, Dr Bennett Omalu, a forensic pathologist. Omalu conducted research on brain damage among American football players. The National Football League officials were not happy with the findings and wanted to stop the film. I watched Will Smith behave like a Nigerian: confident but subdued. He drove a Mercedes-Benz, a car middle-class Nigerians in their fifties and sixties loved to drive. I am sure Will Smith spent time learning and understanding what it means to be a Nigerian. David Oyelowo and Will Smith show that cultural intelligence predicts creativity. Likewise, I have seen many missionaries and ministers in the United Kingdom and Africa who, in order to bring others to Jesus Christ, have become everything to everyone, so that they can win them to Christ. It was Paul who said, "I became all things to all men in order to bring them to Jesus Christ." We are called to be like that, meeting people where they are before we call them to believe.

As a mission director in my former church in Nigeria, we organised many crusades in the rural areas. For effectiveness, we normally invited evangelists to speak and to lead the events who understood the rural areas. I found that very helpful; we had a great success with Evangelist Eze, whom we invited to come along with us. He was very competent and confident working in the rural areas. That experience completely changed my faith into a more radical faith. After that experience, the boldness to minister in a foreign land came to me. That was when the journey to my ministry in London began to take shape.

Improving Self-Confidence and Competence in Cross-Cultural Church and Ministry

Embrace a positive attitude toward developing close relationships with individuals from other cultures and the humility associated with learning from them. Open up to them about your need to learn and ask questions about things that are not clear to you. One way to foster such an attitude is to reflect back on your past successes in cross-cultural settings. Consider whether those experiences hold lessons from which you can learn.

Watch movies from other cultures. Films and television programmes are gold mines for cultural information. The writers and producers of these shows almost subconsciously embed their own cultural values and behaviours within their works. If you want to understand British culture, watch British films; if you want to understand Nigerian culture, watch Nollywood movies; American culture, watch Hollywood films. Read books from other cultures. Books are another form of literary expression replete with cultural gems. Travel to other countries. When you do so, do not just stay in the touristy areas but visit deeper into the interior of the country. For instance, if you visit Nigeria but only stay in Ikoyi or Victoria Island, you will miss out on the culture of Nigeria.

Here in the United Kingdom, expressing too much confidence can lead to some challenges as you engage interculturally. Personal space, both social and emotional, is one of the core cultural norms that sociologists look at when separating different culture groups. Individuals in the United Kingdom are near one end of the spectrum, where people expect a good deal of personal space. The phrase we often use is "respect each other's space." Showing too much confidence can sometimes be taken as invading another's space. The fact that people are not expressing themselves does not mean that they lack confidence. Consider a meeting in which you talk on and on to another individual with grandiose thoughts about a subject you have never really studied, while he listens intently, without once correcting or interrupting you. It is only then, after the meeting, that you learn that your listener has a PhD in the very field about which you were speaking! In doing missions and ministries in the United Kingdom, it is important to be very sensitive to the level of confidence we portray so that it does not come across as cockiness. In other countries like Brazil or Nigeria, however, where less physical and emotional personal space is expected, silence may signify a lack of confidence rather than respect. Individuals in these cultures tend to be less guarded and will be much quicker to assert their own knowledge of a given subject. Again, these are simply cultural differences, without any inherent moral value, one way or the other. Nevertheless, breaking one of these cultural expectations often elicits deep-seated emotional reactions in individuals. In British society, most people focus more on an individual's competence than on their confidence. While in some other cultures, confidence is more valued than competence.

APPLY

Discussion Questions

1) How does your church environment enhance or hamper attitudes towards cross-cultural competence?

2) How does your home environment enhance or hamper attitudes towards cross-cultural competence?

3) Is it possible to engage in intercultural events constructively without confidence in one's ability to do so?

4) How would you create an environment in your fellowship that encourages and mobilises people for mission and ministry?

5) If your fellowship or certain individuals are lacking in self-confidence and competence, list some practical things you can do to improve this weakness.

RESULTS

Scripture warns us not only to be hearers of the Word but to be doers of the Word. As you spend time living out some of the principles learnt in this chapter, write out below a reflection on how you apply them to practical issues. When next the group comes together, consider sharing with each other your experiences.

PART 2

Cultural Intelligence Knowledge in Cross-Cultural Ministry, Mission and the Workplace

This is your level of understanding about how cultures are similar and different and how this might influence us in loving others just as Christ loved us. Cultural Intelligence Knowledge consists of general cultural knowledge and context-specific knowledge

Chapter 5

General Cultural Knowledge in Cross-Cultural Church and Ministry

PREPARE

The Holy Spirit Comes at Pentecost

When the day of Pentecost came, they were all together in one place. Suddenly a sound like the blowing of a violent wind came from heaven and filled the whole house where they were sitting. They saw what seemed to be tongues of fire that separated and came to rest on each of them. All of them were filled with the Holy Spirit and began to speak in other tongues as the Spirit enabled them.

Now there were staying in Jerusalem God-fearing Jews from every nation under heaven. When they heard this sound, a crowd came together in bewilderment, because each one heard their own language being spoken. Utterly amazed, they asked: "Aren't all these who are speaking Galileans? Then how is it that each of us hears them in our native language? Parthians, Medes and Elamites; residents of Mesopotamia, Judea and Cappadocia, Pontus and Asia, Phrygia and Pamphylia, Egypt and the parts of Libya near Cyrene; visitors from Rome (both Jews and converts to Judaism); Cretans and Arabs— we hear them declaring the wonders of God in our own tongues!" Amazed and perplexed, they asked one another, "What does this mean?" Some, however, made fun of them and said, "They have had too much wine."

Acts 2:13 (NIV)

ENGAGE

Introduction

Individuals with high cultural intelligence do not just know a great deal about one or two other cultures besides their own. Although this is part of cultural intelligence, a significant aspect of cultural intelligence involves a more general knowledge about how cultures differ in broader respects. A financial trader may know the specifics about the relative trading values between the yen and the pound, but this general knowledge aspect of CQ involves knowing how a capitalistic economy differs from a socialistic one. Likewise, ministers or missionaries may know the specifics about the different cultures they are serving, but how their own culture differs from the one that they are serving is what this aspect of cultural intelligence explores. Also under this umbrella of general cultural knowledge comes the knowledge of large-scale political systems. This would involve things like knowing how a monarchy differs from a democracy or how Shariah law works in Middle Eastern countries.

Some cultures have very deep-seated role expectations when it comes to males and females. It is often common for Westerners who have experienced the results of a strong cultural backlash against such traditional roles, with the feminist movement, to have a strong negative reaction when encountering a culture with such established roles. The common tendency is to try to cram decades of arguments about the rights and abilities of women into an hour-long argument. The point of cultural awareness and cultural sensitivity is to be able to recognise such deep-seated differences, acknowledging that they are beliefs developed over a lifetime of experiences and are not apt to be changed by one conversation with a foreigner. A friend of mine was surprised when we went to a village church in Nigeria, where men were seated in one place and women in another. In some parts of Asia, you can see a lot of these cultural differences in worship houses. As a minister, it is always helpful to be aware of these differences.

It cannot be emphasised enough that these are deep-rooted philosophies and beliefs that govern how individuals view the world. Recognising that some cultures differ in these fundamental respects allows individuals with high cultural intelligence to be sensitive to the possibility of such differences and to pick up on them when contextual clues indicate that there might be a difference in one of these areas. Our different cultures shape the way we see the world and read and interpret the Bible. They also determine the kind of theology we practice. (See our documentary film, entitled "From theology2theologies")

The Role of Language in General Cultural Knowledge

One of the best ways of developing general cultural knowledge is by learning a second language (or, better yet, a third). The process of learning a second language often teaches the learner about how much their own language impacts and colours the way they perceive the world. Foreign languages always have grammatical rules that cause the learner to think about language in general, in ways they never have before. General cultural knowledge comes from recognising the broader implications that follow from learning another language. A word that I may think of as having a set number of meanings has a different but overlapping set of meanings in this new language I am learning. Therefore, the categories into which I group things are governed by the structures of my English language. Someone speaking Swahili may lump things into entirely different, but consistent, categories that conform more to the structures of that language.

Language is indeed the linchpin of culture. It is not equivalent to culture, but it is integrally tied to it. It is virtually impossible to immerse oneself in another culture without learning the language of that culture as well. It simply cannot be done. There are too many aspects of the culture that tie in with language and require at least a rudimentary understanding of it. This is the reason David Livermore (2011, 98) recommends learning a foreign language as one of the best ways to improve your cultural intelligence.

Since cultural intelligence is a factor that stands apart from specific cultural knowledge (in this particular aspect), it is possible to measure CQ levels before someone learns a second language. Two researchers in Iran had this question and wondered whether a high CQ would be a predictive factor as to which foreign language students would learn to write the best (Ghonsooly and Shalchy, 2013). They studied 104 Iranians who were learning English and gave them a CQ test. They then tested three aspects of their English writing ability: fluency, accuracy, and complexity. What they found was that those participants with the highest cognitive CQ scores were the most likely to have a higher level of fluency in their writing of English. But participants' CQ scores did not correlate to their accuracy or complexity in writing English.

The researchers do not speculate on why writing accuracy or complexity would not be correlated with cognitive CQ, but the answer is not hard to sort out. The complexity of one's writing relates to structural depth of thought in the foreign language. This structural depth is not something you can simply pick up on from observational cues. Similarly, writing accuracy relates to how well one has learned the rules of grammar. There is no reason to think that those with a high CQ would learn the rules of grammar any better or worse than other students. But fluency in writing involves grasping the style and flow of the language. It involves knowing what structures sound more natural than others. It is these types of clues that culturally sensitive individuals are able to pick up on and use. I have met people from other countries who have spent only a few months in the United Kingdom, and they speak and write the English language fluently, while some who have been here for over fifteen years are not so fluent.

Foreign Language Learning and the Gospel Message

It is important to remember that the Christian message is not bound to a single language. This is not true for all religions. In Islam, one cannot translate the Quran into another language. It is forbidden in the faith system itself. The fear is that something will become lost in translation, which is an understandable fear, given how bound up with language culture is. Since religion is a cultural phenomenon, religious ideas are very closely tied to the language they are set in. It is precisely for this reason that Islam does not allow the Quran to be translated.

The Christian tradition presents us with an entirely different take on language. The Christian tradition, first of all, has its roots in the Old Testament, what the Jewish tradition calls the Hebrew Bible. Nevertheless, the Hebrew Bible itself has large sections of the books of Daniel and Ezra that are written in Aramaic, not Hebrew. Several centuries before Jesus' birth, most Jews were reading translations of the Bible in Aramaic (Targumim), and others were reading the Bible in Greek (the Septuagint). It was only a small handful of the most learned rabbis who learned to read and write Hebrew. The Jewish faith was not tied to a particular language—though it retained the position that the authority of the scriptural text remained in the original language.

Jesus spoke Aramaic, and yet the Gospel writers did not feel compelled to preserve all of Jesus' words in Aramaic. In fact, there are only a handful of words preserved in Aramaic within the Gospels, which were written in Greek, along with the remainder of the New Testament. But long before the good news of Jesus' message was presented in Greek, it was restricted to his Aramaic-speaking disciples and the crowd of five thousand to whom he appeared after his resurrection, likely also Aramaic speaking. This was long after Aramaic had ceased to be the international language that united the ancient Near East in trade and commerce. So how did the message spread? Here was where the Holy Spirit stepped in and provided a supernatural solution to a common human problem. The Feast of Weeks in Jerusalem provided the perfect opportunity for spreading the Gospel message. Thousands of Jews from all over the known world had travelled to Jerusalem.

It was then that the Holy Spirit stepped in with supernatural force and provided the gift of tongues to the apostles. Each of the 120 believers who were gathered in that upper room instantly became fluent in another language. They then spread through the crowd, sharing the news of Jesus's death and resurrection to those who had travelled to the festival. This was the spark that would spread Christianity throughout the entire Western world in the coming centuries.

As the church grew, Latin became the new international language and the language of the educated upper class. By the time of Martin Luther, the Latin Vulgate (a late-fourth-century Latin Bible translation) had become the language in which Christian scholars and priests studied both Old and New Testaments. Part of the Reformation teaching was that the Bible belonged to the people and should be translated into their own language. The Reformers understood the importance of the "language of the heart." This is your native language, the language in which you laugh and love and dream and cry. Even for priests who spent years reading Latin, hearing the Bible in their native language was a profound thing. The Reformers were not trying to diminish the value of learning Latin or Hebrew or Greek for understanding the Bible. But more than anything else, they wanted people to be able to hear the Bible in their own heart language. The publication of Martin Luther's German translation of the Bible was one of the pivotal events of the Reformation. In so doing, Martin Luther reminded us that Christianity is not a religion tied to any particular language.

General Cultural Knowledge and the Problem of Translation

One of the reasons why language is a helpful focal point for understanding general cultural knowledge is that it highlights deeper philosophical differences. Calling the head of your country a king, a prime minister, a president, or even a dictator has certain implications beyond language. Our English language divides these into neat categories, but you could not translate these words into ancient Greek—the concepts didn't exist. Oftentimes, concepts in one culture are not present in another. When one culture encounters such a foreign concept, it has several options. It may come up with a phrase that describes the concept or a catchword that captures a part of the concept and applies it to the whole. More often, the language will produce a *calque* or a loanword from the language where the concept originates. Words like "television" and "computer" are quite common in many foreign languages, where the speakers simply adopted the English word. In France, there is actually a society (*Académie Française*) formed with the intention of preserving the integrity of the language; they do not allow such foreign loanwords. They will go to great lengths to form native French words for such foreign concepts or inventions and try their best to discourage other French speakers from using the borrowed forms of the words.

For missionaries to be successful, they have to learn the language of the place where they are going to serve. This is the first step and very important; if I am unable to speak English, my ministry in the United Kingdom will be ineffective. Apart from speaking the language, accent also matters for some people. During a Pentecost festival Sunday worship service, I asked many people from different countries to share prayers in their own languages. It was good to hear them all pray in different languages, though we did not understand what they said, but we were united together by the fact that we were praying to a God who understands all languages. Though different, the understanding of One God helped us say, "Amen," to the prayers, even when we did not understand the language.

Improving Your General Cultural Knowledge and Cognitive Cultural Intelligence

Business/Cultural Systems

1. Pray and ask for divine revelation from the Holy Spirit.

2. Study other cultures; visit or read about other cultures.

3. Google smarter.

4. Improve your global awareness. Use BBC's country profiles.

Interpersonal/Cultural Values

5. Go to the movies or read a novel.

6. Learn about cultural values.

7. Explore your cultural identity.

Socio-Linguistics

8. Study a new language.

Leadership

9. Seek diverse perspectives.

10. Recruit a CQ coach.

Source: (How to improve your general cultural knowledge) Livermore, David. 2011. *The Cultural Intelligence Difference: Master the One Skill You Can't Do Without in Today's Global Economy.* New York.

Another helpful way in which to improve your CQ knowledge (although the research is market-driven) about other cultures is by studying the Globe cultural dimensions; they are helpful in understanding other global cultures.

GLOBE Cultural Dimensions

Global Leadership and Organizational Effectiveness Research was conceived by Robert J. House of the Wharton School of Business University of Pennsylvania looking at how culture relates to organisation and leadership effectiveness. In this book I have applied the different cultural dimension research findings to how it might affect church organisation and it's leadership.

The following dimensions emerged from the Globe research: Please note that these cultural dimensions are just guides as to how a community might behave.

1) High and low performance orientation; the degree to which people or fellowship value rewards. Societies or churches with high performance fellowship are competitive and value feedback. In most of these churches, you don't find many people who want to serve, as they are afraid of failure. Few people who are educated serve within the fellowship. Low performance is the reverse. Churches with this culture do not really care who does what, as long as you are happy to offer yourself to serve. Members are not afraid to serve, because they do not fear failure.

2) High and low uncertainty avoidance fellowship: this is the extent to which a community avoids uncertainty or risk. There are churches with the culture of risk taking. They do not plan for any major events or investments, they just believe that they can, and they go for it. Sometimes they fail; sometimes they win. On the other hand, others plan ahead so as to be able to avoid any uncertainty in the future. Imagine coming from a church where everything is planned months before the time into a fellowship where no planning is done. You would conclude that nothing can be done. I remember sharing with some of our leaders many years ago: about planning ahead, a particular leader would say "if God permits"; the thinking was that we are not even sure if we will get to that day.

3) High and low power distance fellowship. This is the degree to which power is shared within the church community. In a high power distance community, power is concentrated on one person or few people. I was a Catholic during my secondary school days and a former Pentecostal member during my university days, and now I am a Baptist. I know the differences. I understand very well the way power is shared within these three denominations. It can be very frustrating for somebody moving from one denomination to another without understanding the differences. While the pastor and the priest are very powerful within most Pentecostal and

Catholic Churches, it is often not like that in the Baptist Church, where church members meeting is the highest authority. Imagine coming from a church where the pastor is the most powerful and you then find yourself in the Baptist Church. You would not like to attend a church business meeting where the pastor is challenged and sometimes voted out. Likewise, if you are moving from a Baptist church into a Catholic church, you might be frustrated that you do not have a say in what goes on within the church.

4) High and low future orientation community. This is the extent to which a community plans for the future or lives for now, with a "tomorrow will take care of itself" attitude. I know of many fellowships or individuals whose activities, events, and expected results are focused on today and now. Because of resources and culture, most minority churches are short-term oriented in planning, although there are other fellowships that would plan by building solid structures that will outlive them. Imagine that you are a leader from a short-term-oriented culture, and you are leading a long-term-oriented fellowship. You would never understand why people are always setting up committees and holding meetings all the time. The reverse too can be frustrating, as people might think that the church has no focus.

5) High and low assertive community. This is the extent to which people or fellowships are confrontational and aggressive in their relationships with others. High assertive people or fellowships are very direct and competitive in communication. I remember visiting a church in London when I was off work. I was shocked to hear how the pastor was talking about a particular member during preaching, asking questions of another member present at the sermon. In low assertive fellowship, where I have spent most of my time in the United Kingdom, the majority of people are the opposite. Most people value their space and would not want others to step into their private space.

6) Gender egalitarianism. This is the extent to which a church recognises gender inequality and takes steps to correct it. There are some churches where men take the lead in everything and also

a few other places where women take the lead. It is always good to recognise this gender imbalance and make sure that it is addressed. One of the questions I have heard people ask is, "Why are men disappearing from the church?" To what extent is our worship culture feminine in its nature? Might this be a contributing factor, or perhaps more men are losing their faith.

7) High and low humane orientation. This is the extent to which churches or people are humane in their character. The extent to which fellowships care and look out for each other. There are some churches that are very rule and law focused; they judge quickly, and you are easily condemned for committing a sin. Jesus Christ always encouraged his followers to love their neighbour as themselves. Some churches or people can be so humane that they forget that they follow a Holy divine God who is not limited by time and space. A balance is needed between high and low.

8) Individualism versus collectivism. The Globe research identified institutional and in-group collectivism. This is the extent to which people have their sense of identity as either a "we" identity or an "I" identity. There are some churches that see the church as a closely knit family; that we are, because Christ called us into this family. We are now one family. We are one in Christ. In other churches, they might value individual space. I remember joining a congregation when I newly arrived in the United Kingdom. One Sunday, I met somebody from a culture different to my own: we talked and shared together. On the following Wednesday, when I saw the same member on the high street, I greeted him but, to my surprise, his response was very different to Sunday's. I now understand better. It is good to recognise these characteristics in a congregation and learn to adjust and share Christ's love. We are all unique and different. Our differences must not stop us from worshipping together. We must seek to understand our differences and continue to share the love of Jesus Christ.

As you move from one country to another, you will find that there are different cultural clusters. The Globe research lists Sub-Saharan Africa as collective and humane. However, there are a lot of variations between and across these clusters. For instance, in Sub-Saharan Africa, in my own experience and also from speaking to people of different social classes from different parts of Africa over the last ten years, I have come to conclude that middle class and upper middle class Africans have cultural values that are increasingly individualistic, competitive, and narrowed down to the nuclear family and less towards the community. The Ubuntu concept is less treasured in these social classes compared to those in the lower social classes.

APPLY

Discussion Questions

1) What are some cultural opposites that you can think of between different cultures (economic, political, personal, social interactions, etc.)?

2) Can you think of some specific examples where you have seen these general patterns play out?

3) Have you spent time learning a foreign language before? Can you recall any insights you gained into the cultures that speaking that language which emerged from your language learning experience?

4) What foreign language would help you the most in your business or in your personal family interactions?

5) Identify language learners using this game: Have everybody stand; ask those who speak four languages to sit down; three follows, and two, then one.

6) Discuss among your group the cultural dimensions that exist in your church; is your church a high power distance fellowship or low?

7) Go through the other cultural dimensions above and explore what is at play in your church or ministry. Is it helpful or does something need to change?

RESULTS

Scripture warns us not only to be hearers of the Word but to be doers of the Word. As you spend time living out some of the principles learnt in this chapter, write out below a reflection on how you apply them to practical issues. When next the group comes together, consider sharing with each other your experiences.

Chapter 6

Context-Specific Knowledge in Cross-Cultural Church and Ministry

PREPARE

Paul's Plea for Onesimus

Therefore, although in Christ I could be bold and order you to do what you ought to do, yet I prefer to appeal to you on the basis of love. It is as none other than Paul—an old man and now also a prisoner of Christ Jesus— that I appeal to you for my son Onesimus, who became my son while I was in chains. Formerly he was useless to you, but now he has become useful both to you and to me.

I am sending him—who is my very heart—back to you. I would have liked to keep him with me so that he could take your place in helping me while I am in chains for the gospel. But I did not want to do anything without your consent, so that any favor you do would not seem forced but would be voluntary. Perhaps the reason he was separated from you for a little while was that you might have him back forever— no longer as a slave, but better than a slave, as a dear brother. He is very dear to me but even dearer to you, both as a fellow man and as a brother in the Lord.

So if you consider me a partner, welcome him as you would welcome me. If he has done you any wrong or owes you anything, charge it to me. I, Paul, am writing this with my own hand. I will pay it back—not to mention that you owe me your very self. I do wish, brother, that I may have some benefit from you in the Lord; refresh my heart in Christ. Confident of your obedience, I write to you, knowing that you will do even more than I ask. And one thing more: Prepare a guest room for me, because I hope to be restored to you in answer to your prayers.

Philemon 1:8–22 (NIV)

ENGAGE

Introduction (Insider versus Outsider Understanding)

General cultural knowledge about broad generalities and differences between cultures can only get you so far. This type of general cultural knowledge is by its very nature an outsider's perspective (what researchers call an "etic" perspective). It requires comparing and contrasting aspects of one culture with the aspects in another and articulating the similarities and differences (mainly the differences). At some point, the knowledge needs to be about the specific cultural attitudes and beliefs of a particular culture or subculture. The knowledge needs to come from an insider's perspective (what researchers call an "emic" perspective) of another culture. Such an insider's view requires a level of empathy that goes well beyond the more abstract "head knowledge" involved with general cultural knowledge and moves into the realm of "heart knowledge."

Context-specific knowledge may be something as simple as, for example, the fact that most Indian dishes are not made with beef and that one should not expect to be served beef at an Indian restaurant. But this context-specific knowledge moves even deeper than that and recognises the cultural and religious reasons behind the general absence of beef from the Indian diet. These stem from a general belief in the sacred nature of the cow and a reverence for it. Although this information is quite broad and general, it is still context-specific in the sense that it relates to a particular culture and particular set of beliefs and behaviours.

This example is a good one to start with, because as Christians, we do not share this religious belief and may find it contrary to our own beliefs.

Nevertheless, respecting this belief in others is something that we can easily do. It does not present the same difficulty as the Corinthian churches faced in the first century when they were frequently offered meat sacrificed to idols (1 Corinthians 8). Imagine how the Christians who grow up in India interact with their friends. They recognise on a deep level the respect that the Hindu tradition holds for cows and would be familiar with all of the restrictions that this might entail. Not serving beef in a meal or not wearing that new leather coat would likely be second nature to Indian Christians. These Christians can respect their fellow Indians' beliefs while still remaining faithful to their own religious beliefs and tradition and we should be able to do the same.

In some cases, the context also has a subcultural element to it. Business meetings have different protocols from classroom teaching, which in turn differs from that of missionary settings or from peacekeeping groups. Understanding norms and expectations in a particular context involves not only understanding the cultural aspects, but also the subcultural dynamics as well. For instance, as a preacher, I am fully aware that if I am going to preach in a black Pentecostal church, I need to raise the tone of my voice and preach with passion. If I do the same in an English Baptist church, people might be turned off. When I am preaching outside of my church, I have learnt to ask the question, "What is the makeup of your congregation?" Not because I want to change my message but because I want to figure out how to connect cross-culturally so that many in the audience will be carried along.

Paul and Philemon

We mentioned at the beginning of this book that the Apostle Paul was the embodiment of high cultural intelligence. One instance of his reliance on his context-specific cultural knowledge was in the carefully crafted letter to his friend, Philemon. In Ephesus, Paul found himself in prison yet again for preaching the Gospel. While he was there, he was visited by one of his friend's slaves, Onesimus, who was in trouble for something (unspecified) that he did. Roman slave laws allowed that a slave, under threat of serious punishment or death, could legally flee to a friend of his master who held higher social status than his master and plead his case before the master's friend (Seneca, *On Anger*, 3.40.2–4).

Onesimus had travelled from Colossae to Ephesus to plead with Paul while he was in the Roman prison. The Roman authorities there recognised Onesimus' legal right to do this and did not interfere. As he poured his heart out to Paul, Paul shared the Gospel with him and converted Onesimus (1:10). They apparently talked at great length, and Paul found many ways in which Onesimus could aid him while he was in prison (1:1–13). Paul decides to lean on his friend, Philemon, to forgive Onesimus and to actually free him—and lean on him, he does.

In this short letter, Paul uses every conceivable high-sounding means at his disposal to convince Philemon to release Onesimus. Paul, as a Jewish Roman citizen, has an integral knowledge of the slavery system in the Roman Empire and knows what it will take for Philemon to free and release Onesimus from slavery. Paul addresses Philemon from every different cultural avenue he can think of. First, and foremost, he addresses Philemon as a fellow Christian throughout the letter ("our dear friend and fellow worker" [1:1]; "I heard about your faith in the Lord Jesus and your love for all the saints" [#:5]). But while doing so, he also reminds Philemon, in not so subtle ways, that Roman law allows him to command Philemon, as his social inferior, to release Onesimus: "I could be bold and order you to do what you ought to do" (1:8) and "confident of your obedience" (1:21). He also appeals to what we might call a sense of guilt, by saying basically that you should be helping me here while I languish in prison, but since you can't (or won't), Onesimus will make a good substitute (1:13). But in all of this emotional appeal, Paul does not forget the real financial costs and motivations involved in this case. Therefore he says, "If he owes you anything, charge it to me. ... I will pay it back" (1:18–19), carefully paralleling this financial debt with the nonfinancial debt that Philemon owes to Paul ("you owe me your very self" [1:19]) for his conversion.

We have every reason to believe that this letter succeeded in freeing Onesimus. Later, Paul actually sends Onesimus back to Colossae as an ambassador, accompanying his letter to the church there (Colossians 4:9), and later Christian tradition maintains that Onesimus became the first bishop of Ephesus (Ignatius, Letter to the Ephesians, 1:3; 6:2). Paul did not have to try to set Onesimus free. But once he decided that was the course of action he was going to take, he used every bit of his accumulated knowledge about Roman slave culture to make that happen.

Increasing Your Knowledge of Other Cultures

The world is a big place! No one needs to tell you that. But as such, there is simply no way for one person to understand all of the world's cultures and know how best to interact in any cultural setting. But such a daunting task is not what we need to concern ourselves with. We are blessed enough to have various individuals in our lives from different cultural backgrounds. One way to begin increasing our context-specific cultural knowledge is by identifying those cultures we interact with the most, whether it be that of our in-laws, family friends or church members. Once we have identified the particular culture we want to study, it is then just a matter of actively learning about it. We can read novels that are set within that culture. We can also ask questions of our friends or loved ones that give us further insights into their culture.

Also we should pray and ask for divine revelation and the spirit of discernment. Learn to observe, listen and do not jump to conclusions. I suggest taking cultural competence training/workshop.

During one of the cultural competence workshops I organized, one of the participants shared this with us:

> "Several years ago, a group of Korean students visited the church I was in; we had an older Korean man working with us at the time. We invited this group back to our house for coffee, and when they arrived, we had some difficulty in getting them to tell us what they wanted to drink. Having got orders from everybody, we made the drinks and served them. Each of the Koreans seemed almost reluctant to take the drinks and did so with both

hands and with a bow. We discovered later that the awkwardness had been because it is very unusual for an older person to serve a younger person in Korean society and even more so for a perceived church leader to serve church members in this way. We discovered that the students had found this embarrassing. This raises two points: First, we should have known more about Korean attitudes before they arrived; and second, as they were guests in our house, they should have been better briefed before they arrived. The postscript to this is that we had contact over a few days with another group of Korean students this year. They had clearly been properly briefed and had no problems with adapting to Western customs and Western food."

He also shared another story about a pastor who invited a Korean trainee pastor to his home for a meal. In a break in the conversation, the pastor blew his nose. The Korean trainee found this shocking, as this act would be regarded as almost obscene in Korean society. Once we recognise that what we might find very strange can be a result of cultural differences, we are then in a position to walk alongside people from other cultures.

In view of the tropical climate, Africans for example naturally spend more time outdoors, and their talking can be loud. Those from a different culture may perceive them as being too noisy and "in their face": as a result, they may want to disengage from them. Understanding that some people just talk this way, and without intending to frighten or devalue others, helps. An awareness on both sides might help each readjust and make the interaction a healthy one.

What My Principal Taught Me in College

When I arrived in the United Kingdom, I had lots of communication problems with those who engaged in mission with me, despite the fact that I did business with many people from other cultures, especially Americans, who were very direct in their conversations, like Nigerians.

Arriving in the United Kingdom was a different experience for me. In ministry, there were times I acted on what was said, only to see that that was not what was meant. A document included in the table below helped me to navigate how I listened to the locals in my Christian community and the wider community.

During my theological studies in college, our beloved principal gave us a sheet of paper entitled "What most British really mean." According to the paper, it is well known that most British do not always say what they really mean. In cross-cultural missions and ministries, the following table may help people from other nations understand their British counterparts better:

What They Say	What They Mean
I hear what you say.	I disagree and do not wish to discuss it any further.
With the greatest respect ...	I think you are a fool.
Not bad.	Good or very good.
Quite good.	A bit disappointing.
Perhaps you would like to think about ... It would be nice if ...	This is an order. Do it or be prepared to justify yourself.
Oh, by the way ... Incidentally ...	This is the primary purpose of our discussion.
Very interesting.	I do not agree.
Could we consider the options?	I do not like your idea.
I will bear it in mind.	I will do nothing about it.
Perhaps you could give that some more thought.	It is a bad idea, do not do it.
I am sure it is my fault.	It is your fault.
That is an original point of view. That is a brave option to consider.	You must be crazy.
You must come for dinner sometime.	Not an invitation, just being polite.
Not entirely helpful.	Completely useless.

After eleven years of working in the United Kingdom, I have learnt that British people value their privacy, they are tolerant, they value things as they have always been (if it was good for my parents, why should I change it?).

What has worked in the past should not be changed. They value traditions more than big changes and successes. Most take their work very seriously.

APPLY

Discussion Questions

1) Can you think of an example of some context-specific knowledge from another culture with which you are familiar that would be interesting to share?

2) Do you remember any context-specific problems the Jewish Christians had with the Gentile Christians in the early church? Read Acts of Apostles for clues.

3) If you remember one, how was the problem resolved?

4) List all the different ethnic or nationality groups in your church. Share together the different cultural values you know about each culture.

5) Share together challenges and difficulties your congregation has experienced as a result of lack of knowledge of other cultures within your church.

6) How were they resolved?

RESULTS

Scripture warns us not only to be hearers of the Word but to be doers of the Word. As you spend time living out some of the principles learnt in this chapter, write out below a reflection on how you apply them to practical issues. When next the group comes together, consider sharing with each other your experiences.

PART 3

Cultural Intelligence Strategy in Ministry, Mission and the Workplace

Your level of awareness and ability to plan in the light of your cultural understanding.

This part comprises planning, awareness, and checking as it relates to cross-cultural missions and ministries.

Chapter 7

Strategic Planning in Cross-Cultural Church and Ministry

PREPARE

Esther Made Queen

Later when King Xerxes' fury had subsided, he remembered Vashti and what she had done and what he had decreed about her. Then the king's personal attendants proposed, "Let a search be made for beautiful young virgins for the king. Let the king appoint commissioners in every province of his realm to bring all these beautiful young women into the harem at the citadel of Susa. Let them be placed under the care of Hegai, the king's eunuch, who is in charge of the women; and let beauty treatments be given to them. Then let the young woman who pleases the king be queen instead of Vashti." This advice appealed to the king, and he followed it.

Now there was in the citadel of Susa a Jew of the tribe of Benjamin, named Mordecai son of Jair, the son of Shimei, the son of Kish, who had been carried into exile from Jerusalem by Nebuchadnezzar king of Babylon, among those taken captive with Jehoiachin king of Judah. Mordecai had a cousin named Hadassah, whom he had brought up because she had neither father nor mother. This young woman, who was also known as Esther, had a lovely figure and was beautiful. Mordecai had taken her as his own daughter when her father and mother died.

When the king's order and edict had been proclaimed, many young women were brought to the citadel of Susa and put under the care of Hegai. Esther also was taken to the king's palace and entrusted to Hegai, who had charge of the harem. She pleased him and won his favor. Immediately he provided her with her beauty treatments and special food. He assigned to her seven female attendants selected from the king's palace and moved her and her attendants into the best place in the harem.

Esther had not revealed her nationality and family background, because Mordecai had forbidden her to do so. Every day he walked back and forth near the courtyard of the harem to find out how Esther was and what was happening to her.

Before a young woman's turn came to go in to King Xerxes, she had to complete twelve months of beauty treatments prescribed for the women, six months with oil of myrrh and six with perfumes and cosmetics. And this is how she would go to the king. Anything she wanted was given her to take with her from the harem to the king's palace. In the evening she would go there and in the morning return to another part of the harem to the care of Shaashgaz, the king's eunuch who was in charge of the concubines. She would not return to the king unless he was pleased with her and summoned her by name.

When the turn came for Esther (the young woman Mordecai had adopted, the daughter of his uncle Abihail) to go to the king, she asked for nothing other than what Hegai, the king's eunuch who was in charge of the harem, suggested. And Esther won the favor of everyone who saw her. She was taken to King Xerxes in the royal residence in the tenth month, the month of Tebeth, in the seventh year of his reign.

Now the king was attracted to Esther more than to any of the other women, and she won his favor and approval more than any of the other virgins. So he set a royal crown on her head and made her queen instead of Vashti. And the king gave a great banquet, Esther's banquet, for all his nobles and officials. He proclaimed a holiday throughout the provinces and distributed gifts with royal liberality.

Esther 2: 1-18 (NIV)

Further Reading

Esther 3 and 4

ENGAGE

Introduction

As Livermore (2011, 110) explains, CQ strategy forms the transition between CQ knowledge and CQ behaviour. There are many people who have plenty of information about other cultures but who seem unable to put that knowledge into practice. CQ strategy as a whole encompasses the different ways in which individuals use their knowledge to influence their behaviour in cross-cultural situations. Planning is the first element of CQ strategy that warrants discussion.

Planning involves thinking ahead—anticipating what might be involved in an upcoming intercultural situation and preparing for it accordingly. Returning to the literary figure of James Bond, this type of planning is exemplified by Bond's visits to the quartermaster, Q. During these visits, Q undoubtedly explains that his division has anticipated the situations in which 007 will find himself in the upcoming mission. In the light of what they expect, they provide Bond with various gadgets that he might use to get himself out of a jam or to help accomplish a part of his mission. This type of planning parallels the planning that Bond must do that typically does not receive much attention in the stories, as we only see the results. Bond inevitably anticipates the type of cross-cultural setting he will be entering into and relies on past experience, most likely combined with new information that he gathers about the cultural norms and expectations. It is this planning that allows him to be successful in his various missions.

A Specialized Form of Emotional Intelligence

This idea of strategy, with its subcomponent of planning, as an aspect of intelligence relies on previous work on emotional intelligence. As scholars studied IQ, they often came to terms with the stereotypical absent-minded professor—the brilliant individual who was severely lacking in social skills. Scholars recognized that these skills relied on a different aspect of intelligence that was simply located in a different part of the brain. This led them to develop tests for what is now called Emotional Intelligence (EQ), which accesses areas of the brain previously ignored in IQ tests. Cultural intelligence rides on the back of this development in emotional intelligence research and focuses on a particular type of planning that accounts for cultural differences.

Esther and Xerxes

The book of Esther provides another fitting example of the strategic planning element of cultural intelligence. The Persian King Xerxes had been insulted by the behaviour of his primary wife, Vashti, who bore the title of queen. Xerxes' advisors suggested that in the light of the king's displeasure with Vashti, he should strip her of her position as primary wife and queen and should marry another woman, who would take her place, demoting Vashti to his second tier of wives. The search was on throughout the kingdom for a new bride, who would become queen.

Hadassah was a Jewish girl, who had grown up in the Persian Empire. Like the Apostle Paul, who would come many years later, she straddled two different cultures, firmly rooted in her Jewish culture but also fluent in the wider Persian culture, in which she grew up. She, too, had two names, corresponding to the two cultures in which she interacted: her Jewish given name, Hadassah, and her Persian name, the name we know her by, Esther. Upon learning of the king's plan to select a new queen, Esther was one of the women from her district chosen to be considered for the new honour. (Although the king married new women frequently, replacing a primary wife was a rare occurrence.) Now, while Esther was quite familiar with Persian customs in general, she was not familiar with the customs dictated by the royal court and the royal palace. These were the customs she spent learning for over a year, along with lessons in the most current beauty treatments and fashion styles. The level of planning that went into this was great.

This was not the only time we see Esther using her skills at planning in the book. Esther's cousin and adoptive father Mordecai had learned of a plot to kill the Jews throughout the Persian kingdom, which Haman had coerced King Xerxes into signing as law. Mordecai pleaded with Esther to use her political position and her access to the king's ear to change his mind. In so doing, she would make him see the deception Haman used to convince the king to sign the royal edict, which would exterminate the Jews, and her along with it. This was a tricky business, given the expectations and protocols in the palace. In order to succeed, time was of the essence, and Esther needed to gain an audience with the king sooner rather than later. It seems that Xerxes' initial sexual interest in Esther had waned recently, and he was inviting Esther to his bed less and less frequently. This meant that if Esther wanted to speak to the king in time, she would have to initiate such a conversation in the throne room, as opposed to the bedroom. The threat that this posed to Esther was great indeed. If the king had any misgivings whatsoever about Esther approaching him uninvited, it could cost her her life.

In this moment, Esther had to remember all of her training and all of the royal protocols appropriate in this situation. She spent days planning what she would wear and how she would present herself to the king (not to mention garnering a great deal of prayer support along the way). But Esther did not limit her planning to this one moment; she extended it to include throwing a banquet for the king and the plotter, Haman. Such a dinner party is fraught with cultural and social protocols to which the host and guests must adhere. In this act, Esther demonstrates a clear command of all such protocols and a high degree of cultural intelligence.

Strategy Making and Goal Setting

The planning element of strategic cultural thinking involves making the strategy itself. It is the type of thinking that a chess master or military general embodies, the ability to know the person with whom you are engaging and to know what motivates them. This then falls back to the aspects of cultural knowledge discussed in the preceding chapters. Context-specific cultural knowledge requires knowing the broader culture that a person is a part of, along with the smaller subcultural social context in which the interaction will take place. General cultural knowledge helps to fill out general motivations that might be foreign to you and otherwise unanticipated. Planning allows you to anticipate a situation and then turn to a reliable source to learn the culturally expected behaviours within that situation. The reliable source may be a close friend from that culture; it may be a print resource of some type; or it may even be your experience in similar situations within that cultural setting.

Strategic planning involves knowing your own goals in a given intercultural interaction and working out ways in which you might achieve those goals. Many people find such an idea stupid, that one would spend time planning their interactions with other individuals. Some may say this is an act of insincerity and manipulation. But such planning is actually an expression of love and concern for the other person. Think about the amount of planning that one generally puts into a first date. One considers the interests of the other person; the level of interpersonal interaction the activity will allow for; what to wear; back-up plans in the event that something goes wrong; and so on. In a similar way, spending time planning an intercultural interaction and trying to avoid offending or being rude to one's guest is not manipulative but a sign of respect and honour for the other person.

But as everyone knows, plans can only go so far. One can only anticipate so many contingencies. There is always something unexpected that will arise. It is part of the human condition and human nature. We are not robots that can be programmed and relied upon to act predictably. Our behaviour is unpredictable at times. This is where the other elements of CQ strategy come into play. These elements are situational awareness and checking, which will be taken up in the upcoming chapters.

Improving your CQ strategic planning.

When engaging in cross-cultural ministry interactions or mission, plan ahead, think through your meeting and make use of your diary. Plan social interactions and manage expectations. When I first arrived in the UK I was not in the habit of using a diary; all my appointments were stored in my memory. But I soon realised that this would not serve me, as I was working in a culture that took planning ahead very seriously. One of the positive results for me since ministering in the United Kingdom is the ability to plan ahead, using my diary in a constructive way. I know this will be even more helpful as I get older.

Clearly identify what needs to be done, define the issues or problems and find ways to solve the problems before any cross-cultural interactions.

Think about what Jesus said in Luke 6:31: "Do to others what you would have them do to you" when you are planning for a ministry/mission cross-cultural interactions.

When we have done all the planning it is always good to remember that anything can still go wrong as we enter into cross-cultural situations. Be aware, observe and correct anything that is not going well. It is therefore very important that we remember to pray before every planning stage and after.

Planning a Community Festival in Tooting

The area of Tooting and Mitcham, our church's wider community, is a very diverse one, having within it many ethnicities, nationalities, faiths, and age groups. Every year, we had organised a barbecue in our church car park; but in 2011, we organised a community festival at Figges Marsh, a very large common in the area. Our goal was to encourage all the different ethnic and faith groups to enjoy the day together. During our planning, we made sure we clearly understood what would connect with the different cultures we were expecting. We spoke in advance with people from different culture groups to try to establish which activities they would come out for and enjoy doing with others. We had a community relations team who helped to plan our engagement with our diverse community. The festival in 2011 was a success. In 2012 we organised a bigger festival, in which we involved a few other ethnic churches in the area. We made specific plans to involve and accommodate all the cultures within our community and, at the end of the day, it turned out really well for our wider community and us. It was a greater success, even in terms of diversity. We not only had a huge turnout, but people from all the different cultures in our neighbourhood came out for the event. In designing the festival, we spent time studying our community. We partnered with other groups within the community. We had "Share Jesus International" and "Fusion Youth and Community" training before the event. We made sure that volunteers came from the different cultures from within the community. Within our church, we had a congregation of over eighteen nationalities, with all age groups represented. They reached out to their wider communities. We prepared church members to engage one to one with those in our community. We also had three American mission teams to help us on the day.

APPLY

Discussion Questions

1) Can you think of an instance where you spent time planning a social event? How would this planning have changed had there been intercultural elements involved?

2) Do you tend to hold a more negative or a more positive view of the role of planning in social interactions? Have you had experiences that reinforced these beliefs?

3) Read Esther 2. Considering the two situations Esther faced, list the strategic planning actions she embarked on?

4) What could Esther have done differently?

5) Do you take into consideration your self-awareness and the awareness of others when preparing to meet people from other cultures?

6) If yes, list what you would normally look out for.

7) How effective are you in planning to meet people from your culture and those not from your culture?

RESULTS

Scripture warns us not only to be hearers of the Word but also to be doers of the Word. As you spend time living out some of the principles learnt in this chapter, write out below a reflection on how you apply them to practical issues. When the group comes together next time, consider sharing with each other your experiences.

Chapter 8

Mindfulness in Cross-Cultural Church and Ministry

Situational and Self-Awareness in Cross-Cultural Church and Ministry

PREPARE

Solomon's Wives

King Solomon, however, loved many foreign women besides Pharaoh's daughter—Moabites, Ammonites, Edomites, Sidonians and Hittites. They were from nations about which the Lord had told the Israelites, "You must not intermarry with them, because they will surely turn your hearts after their gods." Nevertheless, Solomon held fast to them in love. He had seven hundred wives of royal birth and three hundred concubines, and his wives led him astray. As Solomon grew old, his wives turned his heart after other gods, and his heart was not fully devoted to the Lord his God, as the heart of David his father had been. He followed Ashtoreth the goddess of the Sidonians, and Molek the detestable god of the Ammonites. So Solomon did evil in the eyes of the Lord; he did not follow the Lord completely, as David his father had done.

On a hill east of Jerusalem, Solomon built a high place for Chemosh the detestable god of Moab, and for Molek the detestable god of the Ammonites. He did the same for all his foreign wives, who burned incense and offered sacrifices to their gods.

The Lord became angry with Solomon because his heart had turned away from the Lord, the God of Israel, who had appeared to him twice. Although he had forbidden Solomon to follow other gods, Solomon did not keep the Lord's command. So the Lord said to Solomon, "Since this is your attitude and you have not kept my covenant and my decrees, which I commanded you, I will most certainly tear the kingdom away from you and give it to one of your subordinates. Nevertheless, for the sake of David your father, I will not do it during your lifetime. I will tear it out of the hand of your son. Yet I will not tear the whole kingdom from him, but will give him one tribe for the sake of David my servant and for the sake of Jerusalem, which I have chosen."

1 Kings 11:1–13 (NIV)

"Therefore I tell you, do not worry about your life, what you will eat or drink; or about your body, what you will wear. Is not life more than food, and the body more than clothes? Look at the birds of the air; they do not sow or reap or store away in barns, and yet your heavenly Father feeds them. Are you not much more valuable than they? Can any one of you by worrying add a single hour to your life? And why do you worry about clothes? See how the flowers of the field grow. They do not labor or spin. Yet I tell you that not even Solomon in all his splendor was dressed like one of these. If that is how God clothes the grass of the field, which is here today and tomorrow is thrown into the fire, will he not much more clothe you—you of little faith? So do not worry, saying, 'What shall we eat?' or 'What shall we drink?' or 'What shall we wear?' For the pagans run after all these things, and your heavenly Father knows that you need them. But seek first his kingdom and his righteousness, and all these things will be given to you as well.

Matthew 6:25–33 (NIV)

ENGAGE

Introduction

The idea of mindfulness is what we often talk about as being "fully present" or "in the moment". With our minds always active and thinking about a million different things, it is sometimes difficult to just be present and to focus our attention squarely on our current situation and surroundings. It takes discipline. Although Buddhism places quite a bit of emphasis on this practice, it is certainly not absent from the Christian tradition. I spent one year of training with the Catholic Jesuits in London learning how to find God in all things through reading of scriptures and long meditations. Jesus devoted one section of his Sermon on the Mount to this topic of mindfulness and staying in the present. One distraction that continually takes us out of the present is worry. He gives several admonitions for his disciples not to worry and provides several metaphors to make his point (Matthew 6:25–33). He then concludes the thoughts with this summary statement: "Therefore do not worry about tomorrow, for tomorrow will worry about itself. Each day has enough trouble of its own." (Matthew 6:34).

When we are mindful, we are able to focus our minds on the behaviour, mannerisms, and body language of those around us, as well as notice our own actions and body language and how others respond to it. This mindfulness forms the second element within CQ strategy. The planning takes place before the event, but the mindfulness takes place within the event itself. It allows us to pick up on cues that those around us are perhaps feeling uncomfortable or offended in some way. It keeps us in tune with what is happening around us and allows us to recognize unexpected interactions that our meticulous planning did not (or even could not) account for.

Mindfulness also goes beyond this and involves how we absorb and assimilate what we hear in interactions with others from a different cultural background (Thomas, 2006, 84–85). As we listen mindfully, we create new categories and learn to view problems or ideas with a new perspective. While planning might involve a general sense of the cultural attitudes one might hold, mindfulness allows us to experience more directly how a person feels, what they value, how they behave and expect others to behave, and so on. If we allow ourselves to listen empathetically to others, it opens up a whole new perspective from which we can view the world. This empathy allows us to further interact with others in a respectful and caring way.

Neural scientists studying this idea have actually identified distinct areas of our brain that operate when we focus attention on others and are mindful of them and their actions and when we focus our attention on our own actions and are being self-aware (Rockstuhl et al., 2010, 6–7). The specifics are not important in this context, but the practical implications of this are significant. What this means is that mindfulness is a discipline that must be trained and developed, just like playing the piano or learning calculus. Initially, this behaviour is difficult, because we are not used to accessing this area of our brain. The more we practice mindfulness, the more we strengthen the neural pathways in this section of our brain and can bring more resources to bear in interpreting and understanding the present, and the easier this practice becomes.

Self-Awareness and Core versus Flexible Values

A related aspect of CQ that is best addressed in this context is the idea of core values and beliefs, as contrasted with flexible values and beliefs (Middleton, 2014). What are some of those core values we should hold on to and the others we can be flexible about? As we learn to interact more and more with others from different cultures, it is important, especially as Christians, to be able to identify and differentiate our core values, which define us and make us who we are, from our flexible values and beliefs, which we hold but are willing to bend on in different social contexts. This issue was the one that the early church faced in the Jerusalem Council, discussed earlier in the introductory lesson. As the Jewish Christian community that Jesus had begun started to expand beyond its cultural roots, the question of core versus flexible became quite poignant. Which practices and beliefs were essential to the Christian message and faith and which were simply manifestations of the Jewish context in which the Gospel message originated?

Read Acts 15:1–20.

In her discussion of this context, Julie Middleton (2014) gives a quite striking example of where this question might come up in an intercultural setting. In a Japanese setting, you are expected to bow frequently as a sign of deference. Western tradition often considers this practice offensive. Western heroes and literary figures frequently make comments to the effect that, "I bow the knee to no man." But is this belief an essential part of our identity as human beings, or is this belief something we would be willing to set aside in a context where it was expected as a matter of course? Even if we can dismiss this idea as not necessarily central to our identity as Christians, this does not mean that it might not be central to our identity as a whole. These are not easy questions, but they are essential to work out and answer before getting into a situation where one is put on the spot, without having the opportunity to think it through. I have known individuals who have found themselves in such situations and have regretted their actions in them, because they did not have a chance to think it through beforehand.

This was clearly a problem for early missionaries, who often erred on the side of assigning too many of their beliefs and behaviours to their core, and continues to be a question that modern missionaries repeatedly ask themselves. One helpful way to get a bearing on essential Christian values is by interacting with Christians from another culture. If the Japanese Christians have no problem bowing regularly, this may be a good indication that bowing versus not bowing is not a central tenet within the Christian faith; that understanding prevents us from trying to justify our cultural beliefs by relying on religious reasons that do not actually apply.

Solomon and His Foreign Wives

The Old Testament records a famous situation where an individual did not differentiate his core from his flexible and seriously compromised his values. We have mentioned previously that King Solomon, like his father David, had a very high CQ. He interacted brilliantly with multiple dignitaries from around the ancient world and impressed them with the grace and intelligence he displayed in such intercultural interactions. A part of the protocol involved in such royal interactions was to accept marriage proposals to solidify alliances with various nations. The text of Kings (11:1–13) tells us that he accepted many such proposals, allying Israel with the major political powers of the day. The problem was that, in so doing, he was going directly against a command God had given to the Israelites through Moses (Deuteronomy 7:3).

The problem for Solomon with these marriages was that these foreign wives did not worship the God of Israel, but worshipped multiple other gods from their various cultures. The fear God expressed as a reason for issuing this prohibition was that having parents who worshipped different gods would confuse the children and cause them to stray (Deuteronomy 7:4). But such an arrangement proved to be disastrous for Solomon himself, not just his children, as he worshipped these other gods and goddesses with his wives and even built sanctuaries and temples dedicated to them. But, reflecting back, we may find the source of the problem in David, who married foreign wives as well.

This was clearly a case where Solomon failed to identify his core values before interacting with other cultures. He compromised his values, and God (and later generations of Israelites) judged him for it. But noting that he is carrying on a tradition modelled for him by David, it may be that he put plenty of time and thought into his decision to take foreign wives and used his father's actions as justification for his own actions, as God feared would happen.

Improving Your Mindfulness

David Livermore (2011, 114–125), a Christian author who has written widely on the concept of cultural intelligence, gives four concrete ideas about how to improve your mindfulness. His first suggestion is to "Notice; don't respond" (115–116). The idea is to give yourself time to assimilate new information. Instead of allowing yourself a gut reaction that you may later regret, force yourself to take some time to evaluate what you have just learned or witnessed. His second suggestion is to

"Think widely" (117–119). His point with this suggestion is that most people take on a very large category of incorrect beliefs and behaviours, along with a similarly large category of correct beliefs and behaviours, without an absolute value judgement. By examining your core and flexible values with an eye to critically examining your core and moving those values and beliefs that can legitimately be moved into flexible, you will find yourself more empathetic with those from other cultural contexts. Livermore's third suggestion is one we have already covered in some depth, which is to "Focus deeply" (120–122). By this, he is referring to developing your mindfulness and ability to be present in the moment. His fourth suggestion is to "Journal" (write down), which relates to self-awareness (123–125). Journaling is a good way to get in touch with your own feelings, attitudes, and beliefs and to address them thoughtfully and critically.

One thing I noticed early on in London was the level of preparation people would put into cross-cultural missions and ministries before they engaged. During my first ministry in the United Kingdom, at most meetings I attended with people from other cultures, I discovered that I was always behind in the conversations, because I was trying to process what was being discussed, whilst the others moved to another topic on the agenda. For a few weeks, I did not know what was going on with me until I realised that it was my lack of preparation before the meeting. While those from other cultures spent time preparing and having informal discussions before the meeting, I waited for the meeting itself and just turned up. I finally discovered that I needed to spend more time preparing and researching what was on the agenda. As a mission director in Nigeria, we did more planning for events than preparations for meetings. While this worked in one particular cultural context, it did not work in another.

When engaging in cross-cultural interactions, observe everything happening around you. When engaging in cross-cultural mission or ministry, never make any judgement. There is a saying, "Never judge a book by its cover." So it is with any cross-cultural interactions; observe, learn from your observations, and reflect on them, including the possibility of keeping a journal about them. It is very important to write down what you observe. It is also important not to let yourself be distracted. Full presence of mind, body, and soul is very important in cross-cultural mission and ministry interactions.

APPLY

Discussion Questions

1) Is mindfulness a practice that you have been able to cultivate, or is it an area that you could improve on?

2) Can you think of any instances where your own situational awareness alerted you that an interaction was not quite right?

3) As you continue to engage in missions and ministries, list some of the core values that need not change, if any.

4) Also list flexible values, the ones you are prepared to be flexible about.

5) Discuss Bible principles and instructions that are core and those that you might be flexible about, if any.

RESULTS

Scripture warns us not only to be hearers of the Word but also to be doers of the Word. As you spend time living out some of the principles learnt in this chapter, write out below a reflection on how you apply them to practical issues. When the group comes together next time, consider sharing with each other your experiences.

Chapter 9

Strategic Evaluation in Cross-Cultural Church and Ministry

PREPARE

Naomi Loses Her Husband and Sons

In the days when the judges ruled, there was a famine in the land. So a man from Bethlehem in Judah, together with his wife and two sons, went to live for a while in the country of Moab. The man's name was Elimelek, his wife's name was Naomi, and the names of his two sons were Mahlon and Kilion. They were Ephrathites from Bethlehem, Judah. And they went to Moab and lived there.

Now Elimelek, Naomi's husband, died, and she was left with her two sons. They married Moabite women, one named Orpah and the other Ruth. After they had lived there about ten years, both Mahlon and Kilion also died, and Naomi was left without her two sons and her husband.

When Naomi heard in Moab that the Lord had come to the aid of his people by providing food for them, she and her daughters-in-law prepared to return home from there. With her two daughters-in-law she left the place where she had been living and set out on the road that would take them back to the land of Judah.

Then Naomi said to her two daughters-in-law, "Go back, each of you, to your mother's home. May the Lord show you kindness, as you have shown kindness to your dead husbands and to me. May the Lord grant that each of you will find rest in the home of another husband." Then she kissed them goodbye and they wept aloud and said to her, "We will go back with you to your people." But Naomi said, "Return home, my daughters. Why would you come with me? Am I going to have any more sons, who could become your husbands? Return home, my daughters; I am too old to have another husband. Even if I thought there was still hope for me—even if I had a husband tonight and then gave birth to sons— would you wait until they grew up? Would you remain unmarried for them? No, my daughters. It is more bitter for me than for you, because the Lord's hand has turned against me!" At this they wept aloud again. Then Orpah kissed her mother-in-law goodbye, but Ruth clung to her. "Look," said Naomi, "your sister-in-law is going back to her people and her gods. Go back with her."

But Ruth replied, "Don't urge me to leave you or to turn back from you. Where you go I will go, and where you stay I will stay. Your people will be my people and your God my God. Where you die I will die, and there I will be buried. May the Lord deal with me, be it ever so severely, if even death separates you and me." When Naomi realized that Ruth was determined to go with her, she stopped urging her.

So the two women went on until they came to Bethlehem. When they arrived in Bethlehem, the whole town was stirred because of them, and the women exclaimed, "Can this be Naomi?"

"Don't call me Naomi," she told them. "Call me Mara, because the Almighty has made my life very bitter. I went away full, but the Lord has brought me back empty. Why call me Naomi? The Lord has afflicted me; the Almighty has brought misfortune upon me." So Naomi returned from Moab accompanied by Ruth the Moabite, her daughter-in-law, arriving in Bethlehem as the barley harvest was beginning.

Ruth 1:1-22 (NIV)

Further Reading

Ruth 2 and 3

ENGAGE

Introduction

Evaluation completes the strategic aspect of CQ. More commonly known as "checking," evaluation involves a real-time adjustment of the planning aspect of strategy. This is where we can make adjustments to how we approach a cultural situation. In human interactions and social events, things rarely take place exactly as planned. There is always some additional variable or unexpected element to destabilise our plans. Individuals in missions and ministries with high CQ are able to make such mental adjustments on the wing.

The process of evaluation assumes both planning and mindfulness as prerequisites. If there has been no planning, there are no expectations to adjust. If there is no mindfulness, there can be no recognition that the original planned strategy needs adjustment. Referring back to my example in chapter 8, because I did not prepare for meetings ahead of time, I discovered that I was not concentrating well in those meetings. This also meant I could not notice what I needed to change after the meetings. But, when I realised what I was not doing well prior to meetings with people from other cultures, I learned and adapted accordingly. This then helped me to focus and be mindful during those meetings; as a result, I knew and remembered those things I needed to check and correct (in other words, what I did well and what needed to change).

Ruth and Boaz

Ruth was a Moabite who had married into an Israelite family living in Moab. She became a widow when her husband died, which was compounded by the fact that her Israelite mother-in-law, Naomi, was also a widow. Widowhood was the kiss of death for women in ancient Israelite society and often relegated them to abject poverty. The prophets continually passed on messages from the Lord asking the Israelites to care for the orphan and the widow and not to oppress them (Isaiah 1:17; Jeremiah 7:6; 22:3; Zechariah 7:10). Her mother-in-law had probably lived with Ruth and her husband before he passed away, and Ruth still felt a strong sense of responsibility for her. She refused to abandon her mother-in-law and return to her family of origin, where Naomi would not be accepted.

So they travelled to Naomi's homeland, Judah, to live out their lives there. Ruth prepared herself for this cross-cultural experience by learning the Judean customs related to farming. She learned that during harvest season, when the reapers gleaned the harvest, they did not make a second pass and glean what they missed the first time, as they did in Moab. Moses had declared a law he received from the Lord that prevented this second pass (Deuteronomy 24:21). As a widow, Ruth was entitled to glean the remaining barley that the reapers missed. When they reached Judah, Ruth put this into practice and asked the reapers for permission to act according to the law of Moses.

What Ruth did not know (and Naomi had forgotten) was that there was a kinsman-redeemer who lived in Bethlehem, named Boaz. Israelite law allowed for such a kinsman-redeemer to marry Ruth so that she and her mother-in-law would be incorporated into his household. This was an unexpected turn of events for Ruth, and she had to learn more about Israelite culture and law than she knew before. This time, she had to learn about the laws and customs surrounding a kinsman-redeemer. Naomi was more than happy to teach her what she needed to know in this new set of circumstances.

The harvest season was such a busy time for farmers that they did not journey home in the evenings, but slept on the threshing floor, where they could oversee the work that extended well into the evening. They would work in the fields during the daylight hours and otherwise thresh and process the grain after sundown by the lamps at the threshing floor, where they would also drink and toast to the successful harvest season. Naomi knew that the kinsman-redeemer was not required by law to marry Ruth (Leviticus 25:47–49; the laws regarding redeeming someone from debt slavery parallel the case of the widow). But she also knew that Israelite law held that if Boaz slept with Ruth, then he would be obligated to marry her (Deuteronomy 22:28–29). When Naomi tells Ruth to "uncover his feet and lie down" (Ruth 3:4), she is actually telling her to disrobe him and take his clothes off and have sex with him. The term 'feet' is a very common Hebrew euphemism for the genitals and is used in various contexts to refer to the genitals of men or women (Pope, 1992, 720–722, and any standard Old Testament Hebrew dictionary). The Hebrew word for "lie down (with)" is also used frequently as a euphemism for sex (Campbell, 1964, 131–132). He also hurries her out of the building so that no one will discover what has happened between them (Ruth 3:14), which would be an odd behaviour if this had simply been an innocent marriage proposal (which would usually be the cause of celebration). Once Boaz has slept with Ruth, he now feels an obligation to marry her (which is what Naomi was counting on), but he must go through the proper channels. This behaviour was very risky, and it was only because of Naomi's native knowledge of the cultural norms and laws that the plan succeeded.

Ruth had an initial plan for her cross-cultural experience in Bethlehem, and then the expected circumstances changed. Ruth was able to recognize, with Naomi's help, the opportunities and challenges presented by the new situation. She then adjusted her plans and behaviour in light of the new situation. This type of checking or strategic evaluation is a part of cultural intelligence.

Improving Strategic Evaluation Skills

David Livermore (2011, 132–137) gives three concrete exercises that we can use to improve our strategic evaluation skills. He suggests that we 1) reframe the situation; 2) test for accuracy; and 3) ask better questions. Livermore notes that when in a cross-cultural situation, some events will take place that are out of our control. When this happens, it threatens to paralyse us and cause us to lose our bearings. Livermore suggests taking the following steps to prevent such an outcome. The first is to quickly and briefly label the emotion that the event has created. Anger is the emotion that reframing helps to dispel the most. He gives the example of not being able to get clear directions to a hotel. Talking it through or writing it down provides a perspective that can redirect the anger that is often wrongly directed at another person. The second exercise, testing for accuracy, is one that takes place in conjunction with mindfulness. Our perceptions of a situation are not always accurate. Asking a simple question or throwing out a suggestion can sometimes help to confirm or invalidate what we think is happening. We can ask such questions in the moment or later, as we debrief someone else and get their thoughts on the situation and our assessment of it. The third exercise is to ask better questions. Remember the question of bowing in Japanese cultures? When we face an intercultural situation that makes us uncomfortable, the best thing to do is to ask ourselves why, over and over again. Why does bowing make me uncomfortable? Why do I feel that way? Why should this be part of my core values, or why should it be part of my flexible values?

APPLY

Discussion Questions

1) Can you think of other social situations (not necessarily intercultural in nature) where you have noticed something happening outside of the expected and changed your approach or your plans?

2) List the opportunities Ruth encountered and how she made use of them.

3) List the challenges Ruth encountered and how she coped with them.

4) What did Ruth do differently that helped her situation?

5) How can you help immigrants within your congregation or community who may be dealing with serious challenges?

RESULTS

Scripture warns us not only to be hearers of the Word but also to be doers of the Word. As you spend time living out some of the principles learnt in this chapter, write out below a reflection on how you apply them to practical issues. When the group comes together next time, consider sharing with each other your experiences.

PART 4

Cultural Intelligence Action in Ministry, Mission and the Workplace

Your level of adaptability when relating and working inter-culturally

This part comprises verbal behaviour and nonverbal behaviour as it relates to cross-cultural missions and ministries.

Chapter 10

Verbal Behaviour in Cross-Cultural Church and Ministry

PREPARE

Paul then stood up in the meeting of the Areopagus and said: "People of Athens! I see that in every way you are very religious. For as I walked around and looked carefully at your objects of worship, I even found an altar with this inscription: to an unknown god. So you are ignorant of the very thing you worship—and this is what I am going to proclaim to you.

"The God who made the world and everything in it is the Lord of heaven and earth and does not live in temples built by human hands. And he is not served by human hands, as if he needed anything. Rather, he himself gives everyone life and breath and everything else. From one man he made all the nations, that they should inhabit the whole earth; and he marked out their appointed times in history and the boundaries of their lands. God did this so that they would seek him and perhaps reach out for him and find him, though he is not far from any one of us. 'For in him we live and move and have our being.' As some of your own poets have said, 'We are his offspring.'

"Therefore since we are God's offspring, we should not think that the divine being is like gold or silver or stone—an image made by human design and skill. In the past God overlooked such ignorance, but now he commands all people everywhere to repent. For he has set a day when he will judge the world with justice by the man he has appointed. He has given proof of this to everyone by raising him from the dead."

Acts 17:22–31(NIV)

ENGAGE

Introduction

Verbal communication in missions and ministries with others is fraught with certain acceptable and unacceptable modes of behaviour. These modes encompass accent; tone; inflection; speed; volume; warmth; enthusiasm; formality; and pauses and silence. Both cultures and sub-cultures have unspoken expectations about the appropriate range for each of these modes involved in speech. Speaking too loudly or informally in certain contexts can come off as rude or offensive to listeners. Most of us navigate these expectations in our various subcultures with ease. The speech volume that we use when watching a football match is quite different from the volume we might use in a romantic dinner with a spouse. The tone we use to address a professor is markedly different from the tone we might use with a best friend. In Britain, where I currently minister and live, many speak with a low tone of voice; what often surprises me when I watch the same people on television in a football stadium or in the House of Commons is how loud they can be.

I have mastered the art of changing my tone when I preach in different churches. Many years ago, I was invited to preach in a Pentecostal church with Nigerian members; this was not just a one-off but was for many Sundays. However, I was then serving in a white majority church, where my tone of preaching had been conditioned to be low (but probably not as low as many would have wanted it to be). When I got to the Pentecostal church, I preached in a low tone, and many within the audience were very disappointed. I could see it from their faces as I preached, and a few fell asleep! After the service, the pastor of the church, who knew where I was ministering, reminded me that I was not preaching to my usual congregation but to people from my own culture. This was an important observation given that, as Nigerians, we are loud, not just loud, but very loud. Preaching with a low tone was therefore inappropriate for both the Pentecostal and the Nigeria contexts. Thus, I realised that I had not been cognisant of the unspoken rules of acceptable verbal communication within a Nigerian Pentecostal church, choosing unconsciously to preach in a way that was more appropriate to my Baptist congregation. Though the message was good, I did not connect with the culture. Of course, when I went back the following Sunday, the church was "on fire"! If I preached in this way in my church, some might walk out. The issue here is not whether there is a right or wrong way of preaching, but rather, it is about contextualisation; which means making it appropriate to the relevant context you are engaging with.

Just as there are different expectations for these modes of speech in the subcultures in which we move, different ethnic cultures have different expectations in these areas. American college classrooms often use a level of familiarity in speech that would be unheard of in the classroom of an English university. Knowing these rules and expectations is part of context-specific knowledge, an aspect of CQ already discussed. This aspect of CQ focuses on an individual's ability to put this knowledge into practice in intercultural situations. Some individuals know the unspoken expectations of speech in a given context but are unable to adapt their native patterns to the new intercultural context in which they find themselves.

An Example from International Negotiation

Professor Phyllis Bernard (2009) examined the differences between Western and non-Western cultures in the particular subculture of international business relations and, more specifically, in negotiations. One difference she notes was pointed out by the late American anthropologist Edward Hall. He divided cultures into two broad categories that he coined "low context" and "high context" societies. Northern European and North American societies fall into the low context category, whereas Latin American, Middle Eastern, and Japanese cultures fall into the high context category. In the first category, low context, family is very important except during business hours; whereas the second category, high context, sees family connections as an integral part of business life as well as home life. The second category encompasses honour/shame-based cultures, where avoiding shame is more important even than avoiding death.

When it comes to contract agreements, the low context cultures tend to place the most value on written documents, in contrast to the high context cultures, where the unwritten social dynamics take pride of place. Professor Bernard argues that Western businesspeople need to learn to step back from the logic-based approach in which they have been trained and acknowledge the feelings of the other party in the negotiation. Negotiators from high context societies may completely walk away from a contract that is quite advantageous financially if it means they have to lose face in order to sign it. Bernard argues that by incorporating feelings and core beliefs into intercultural negotiations, Western negotiators can better navigate them.

Paul and the Athenians

Paul has figured prominently in this discussion of CQ because he so embodies the qualities that CQ measures. It should be no surprise then that he provides an apt example in this context as well. In the book of Acts (17:22–31), Luke records a speech that Paul delivered to the Athenians when he visited their city. Luke describes the setting in Athens, highlighting the multitude of pagan idols in the city (Acts 17:16) and the natives' propensity for philosophical debates (Acts 17:17–21). It is in this context that Paul addresses what would be our equivalent of the Court of Appeals (the Areopagus) (Acts 17:22).

Here, Paul meets the Athenians on their level. He completely ignores the scriptures that he has quoted without fail in his communications with Jewish Christians. When he quotes a source, it is not Moses or the prophets, but rather the Greek poets (Acts 17:28). Neither does he argue that Jesus is the Messiah prophesied in the scriptures, for this would be meaningless to the Athenians he was addressing. Rather, he takes as his starting point an inscription that he read on one of their idols, "to an unknown god" (Acts 17:23). But then he uses his training in Greek rhetoric to argue his case for God, which was something he never had to broach with his Jewish audiences. Moreover, he does not even mention Jesus, except to cite his resurrection as further proof of monotheism (belief in one God) (Acts 17:31).

What is striking here is the flexibility that Paul displays in such a central belief as the presentation of the Gospel message. He does not have a set five-point message that he pulls out any time he has the opportunity to share the message of Jesus. Rather he is in tune with his audience and their cultural expectations and core belief system. Knowing that his audience does not value the Hebrew Scriptures as authoritative, he does not even bother to make reference to them. He is just as comfortable citing secular authors to make his point.

Improving Verbal Cultural Intelligence

Once again, David Livermore has some ideas for us on how we might improve upon our verbal CQ. Once again, he turns to learning a foreign language, which he notes is a linchpin in cultural intelligence that appears in one form or another in all of the various components of CQ (Livermore, 2011, 155). Ideally, we should become fluent in the languages of the different cultures with which we interact the most. But for most of us, this is not feasible, for various reasons. So Livermore suggests a much more manageable strategy that is certainly do-able for any of us. He suggests that we learn a handful of key words and phrases in the language of the foreign culture with which we interact the most. Words like "please," "thank you," "sorry," "hello," and "goodbye" (Livermore, 2011, 155). As we have mentioned before, people have a very powerful reaction when they hear you speaking their language. It expresses an interest in their culture that most people find very appealing.

A second strategy Livermore suggests is to try new vocal sounds. By this, he covers a wide range of territory. His first suggestion in this regard is to identify your favourite filler phrase: "right," "got it," "uh-huh," or "sure," to name just a few English fillers. Once you have identified it, try either eliminating it or replacing it with a different filler that you do not use often. This exercise allows us to become more comfortable with changing our ingrained speech patterns. Another suggestion he has along these lines is to alter the volume at which you speak. Speaking softly can convey timidity, shyness, or fear, and speaking loudly can convey power, authority, or anger in some cultures, while in some others the reverse might be the case. Again, learning to vary the volume of our speech in our subcultures will make it more comfortable to vary it when interacting in a different cultural setting entirely.

Tooting Junction Baptist Church has a very diverse congregation of about eighteen nationalities. The congregation is made up of people from the Caribbean Islands, White and Black British, Africans, Eastern Europeans, and American. During our week-day prayer meeting sessions, some felt they could not participate fully because of the style of prayer. They suggested that they would like more freedom to pray in a different way, because they were not used to praying in that particular way. As a result, sometimes they stayed away from prayer meetings! We then considered trying an additional prayer meeting strategy, where people could pray more freely and comfortably in a way that was natural to them. When we introduced this it was apparent that particular cultures preferred this prayer meeting choice to the previous one (though it was surprising to note that one could not predict who would necessarily attend which of the two prayer groups - the first prayer group style was quieter and contemplative, while the additional group was louder and more expressive). However, it succeeded in getting more people involved in prayer meetings. When the congregation meets together on Sundays, we vary the way we pray from time to time. We are at a comfortable place today where many are happy to be quiet while others pray out loud, and vice versa.

APPLY

Discussion Questions

1) Do you often notice the tone or accent of others when you interact with them in missions and ministries? If you do, does it make any difference?

2) Do you notice your own tone when interacting with others, and are you able to detect if it makes them comfortable or uncomfortable?

3) If you were asked to prepare a talk for a meeting with black ethnic minority fellowship, what would you take into consideration?

4) If you were asked to prepare a talk for a fellowship with only English members, what would you take into consideration?

5) If you were asked to speak to a congregation with a very mixed audience of Nigerians, English, Americans, Germans, and Egyptians, what would you take into consideration?

6) How do you think Paul was able to connect with his audience in a very profound way? What did he do well?

7) What could Paul have done better, if anything?

RESULTS

Scripture warns us not only to be hearers of the Word but also to be doers of the Word. As you spend time living out some of the principles learnt in this chapter, write out below a reflection on how you apply them to practical issues. When the group comes together next time, consider sharing with each other your experiences.

Chapter 11

Nonverbal Communication in Cross-Cultural Church and Ministry

PREPARE

On Covering the Head in Worship

I praise you for remembering me in everything and for holding to the traditions just as I passed them on to you. But I want you to realize that the head of every man is Christ, and the head of the woman is man, and the head of Christ is God. Every man who prays or prophesies with his head covered dishonours his head. But every woman who prays or prophesies with her head uncovered dishonours her head—it is the same as having her head shaved. For if a woman does not cover her head, she might as well have her hair cut off; but if it is a disgrace for a woman to have her hair cut off or her head shaved, then she should cover her head. A man ought not to cover his head, since he is the image and glory of God; but woman is the glory of man. For man did not come from woman, but woman from man; neither was man created for woman, but woman for man. It is for this reason that a woman ought to have authority over her own head, because of the angels. Nevertheless, in the Lord woman is not independent of man, nor is man independent of woman. For as woman came from man, so also man is born of woman. But everything comes from God.

Judge for yourselves: Is it proper for a woman to pray to God with her head uncovered? Does not the very nature of things teach you that if a man has long hair, it is a disgrace to him, but that if a woman has long hair, it is her glory? For long hair is given to her as a covering. If anyone wants to be contentious about this, we have no other practice—nor do the churches of God.

1 Corinthians 11:2–16 (NIV)

ENGAGE

Introduction

Although in missions and ministries, we tend to focus on the verbal aspect of our communication, whether it be spoken or written, in actuality, 55 percent of our in-person communication is nonverbal, consisting of gestures, facial expressions, and body language (Mehrabian, 1971). Because different cultures have different expectations about appropriate gestures and body language in various social situations, the ability to modify one's nonverbal behaviour to accommodate a different cultural setting is an important component of CQ. Some broad examples of cultural differences in this regard include expectations regarding the distance between individuals; the nature and amount of physical contact; the amount of eye contact; and the type of greeting (handshake, hug, kiss, etc.) (Van Dyne et al., 2012). In African cultures, especially Nigeria, looking into an older person's eyes during conversation is a sign of disrespect; while in other cultures, like in the West, *not* doing this might be misinterpreted as meaning you are not confident or are lying. Some Western cultures believe that when someone talks to you without looking into your eyes, this means they are hiding something from you.

This has been very evident in my ministry. One day, I spoke with somebody who said that, because a young African boy had not been making eye contact whilst talking to him, he must have been lying. When I suggested to him that it may have been a sign of respect, that he was not looking at his face while speaking, he could not understand what I was saying. That was when it dawned on me that nonverbal behaviours can be an important component when engaging in cross-cultural missions and ministries. Another example I noticed in cross-cultural missions is that, when Europeans or Americans speak with Nigerians or other Africans, and the Africans do not understand them because they are talking too fast, the Africans will simply smile or laugh. This may be out of respect; they do not want to disappoint or shame the speaker by saying they cannot follow or understand when they speak too fast. It seems Europeans or Americans find it easier to say, "I cannot hear you," when the other speaks. It is very important that we notice some nonverbal communication going on during our interactions. Some people might misinterpret Africans smiling during a conversation as meaning approval, but that may not necessarily be the case.

A church member shared with me about smiling and how, "In western culture, it could be considered offensive or rude to smile if no joke had been intended" She said, "My former thesis supervisor used to ask me during the first few months of working with him. 'Have I said something funny? so why are you smiling then?' I had to explain to him that I needed to get used to his English but that, culturally, I was not conditioned to telling him I did not understand what he said. We eventually settled well into the routines and have great respect for one another to this day". We also had the example of an Indian student who had just arrived from India, many years ago. He worshipped with us, and, when I preached, he shook his head as if he did not agree with what I was saying. We had a discussion about a particular sermon; I had noticed him shaking his head while I preached. When I discussed it with another friend, he told me that this was a nonverbal communication of approval and not disapproval! The student later told me how much he enjoyed my sermons.

Another important aspect of nonverbal communication is personal grooming and clothing. What we wear and how we groom ourselves conveys a message to those around us. But, unfortunately, the same outfit and outward appearance can convey different messages in different cultural contexts. Whether it be a big business deal or communicating the Gospel message, knowing how different cultures perceive different clothing styles can be important when speaking cross-culturally. In some social situations where casual attire may be completely appropriate and even expected, that same casual attire may appear rude in another culture. A friend was sharing with me about his experience at university in the United Kingdom. He shared a flat with two of his friends, one of whom was Swedish and the other English. Every day he would take time to iron his clothes before wearing them; he bought expensive shoes and clothes; but his friends would just wear their clothes unironed. He was surprised one day when one of his friends asked why he was so vain, saying he focused too much on his clothes and appearance. That was a surprise to him! In ministry, I often notice that when pastors meet in our conferences, many will be formally dressed, while some from other cultures dress very simply. During my early years in missions and ministries, I would dress formally to all my meetings, both formal and informal. I discovered, however, that many of my English counterparts dressed informally in most meeting situations. I had to adapt to this. But it backfired on me on my mission trip back to Nigeria; I dressed informally to a meeting, and somebody thought I had forgotten I was speaking that day! It reminded me that I was in a different setting and I needed to adapt for the next day.

An Example: Paul and the Women of Corinth

In the 50s (not the 1950s but the actual 50s AD), the church at Corinth was having an internal dispute about what to wear to church. The congregation was culturally mixed, with ethnic Greeks and ethnic Romans. In the local Roman culture, clothing was considered very symbolic, and they placed a great amount of weight on the nonverbal message conveyed by clothing (Oster, 1988, 491). This was especially true in Roman religious settings, where head coverings were a regular part of the expected attire for both men and women. The new Roman Christians at Corinth learned of the Jewish cultural expectation that women should keep their head covered (all the time, not just for worship). There was likely little, if any, Jewish presence in the church at Corinth. The letters to the Corinthians hardly make any references to Jews or Jewish traditions (1 Corinthians 9:20 contains one passing reference), in contrast to letters like Romans and Galatians, where references to Jews and Greeks abound. Through the lens of their own cultural expectations, this group developed the hybrid belief that Christian women should cover their heads during worship. (In 1 Corinthians 11:16, Paul acknowledges that this practice is unique to the Corinthian church and absent from all other congregations he has founded). By contrast, first-century Greeks viewed clothing as ornamental—simply a fashion statement. Like Roman women, Greek women occasionally wore head coverings, but they saw no larger message in this fashion choice (Thompson, 1988). This group in the Corinthian church saw absolutely no need for women to cover their head during the worship service. At an impasse, the church wrote again to Paul to help arbitrate the conflict (1 Corinthians 7:1).

In keeping with his general framework for resolving such disputes about church practice (laid out in 1 Corinthians 8–10), Paul must convince the more permissive ethnic Greeks to yield their position to the guilt-ridden Roman believers. To accomplish this, he provides three arguments from creation: the order of creation (11:3–8); the purpose of creation (11:9–10); and the biology apparent in creation (11:11–15).

It is his final argument that shows off Paul's high CQ most clearly. Pastors, theologians, and even biblical scholars have long been puzzled by Paul's appeal to what "the very nature of things" (the NRSV translates "nature itself") teaches (11:14). One of the clearest explanations of Paul's argument here was found by Troy Martin (2004) during his study of Greek medical texts. Basically, Paul is making reference to what each of these first-century Roman citizens (both Greek and Roman) would have learned in their primary school biology classes. Hippocrates and other Greek medical texts describe in great detail what the current understanding of human hair was. These writers describe hair as hollow tubes that act as vacuums for bodily fluid (think reproductive fluid like semen). Shorter hair on men's heads would decrease the amount of suction upwards into their bodies and thus increase their fertility. Inversely, longer hair on women would increase the amount of suction upwards into their bodies, thereby increasing their fertility. In their honour and shame culture, infertility was shameful, whereas fertility was a mark of honour. So advertising one's infertility (a man with long hair) would be disgraceful (11:14), but advertising one's fertility (a woman with long hair) would be honourable (11:15). He shows the ethnic Greeks that, from the viewpoint of the Roman believers, women worshipping in the service with their head uncovered presents the same social statement that the Greek believers interpret when they see a woman with her head shaved (11:6).

As he did with the Athenians, Paul uses cultural knowledge that he shares with his audience to make his liturgical argument. He is meeting them on their own terms, both acknowledging and leveraging their own worldview.

Improving Nonverbal Cultural Intelligence

Two of the strategies that David Livermore suggests with regard to increasing your nonverbal CQ competence seem especially helpful and actionable. One of these is to take a page from an actor's playbook. Actors will follow and study people who embody the role they want to play: a physician; a police detective; or a cut-throat lawyer. They will try to take on their attitudes and concerns for other people and, most importantly, their mannerisms and physical behaviour. They study and then imitate. It is important that imitating them does not take place on the spot, because this comes off as mimicry or mockery. This is in essence what people with high CQ do naturally without even thinking about it, but those of us who are less gifted with CQ may need to be more self-aware about this imitation.

A second idea he suggests is to make certain behaviours or mannerisms taboo for yourself. One example Livermore cites, is handing an item to a person with your left hand. Many cultures consider this offensive. Rather than trying to remember which cultures hold this belief, if we can simply train ourselves to always hand things to others using our right hand, we will avoid offensive behaviour in this regard. For learning the major taboos and social expectations, Livermore recommends the book *Kiss, Bow, or Shake Hands* (1994).

APPLY

Discussion Questions

1) List the different nonverbal communications you have noticed with specific cultures in your congregation.

2) How do you plan to adapt to these different nonverbal gestures?

3) What was the problem in the church in Corinth?

4) How did Paul go about correcting the problem in the church?

5) If you were in Paul's position, what would you have done?

6) Are there similar situations in your church today that might be causing problems? How would you solve them?

RESULTS

Scripture warns us not only to be hearers of the Word but also to be doers of the Word. As you spend time living out some of the principles learnt in this chapter, write out below a reflection on how you apply them to practical issues. When the group comes together next time, consider sharing with each other your experiences.

Chapter 12

Recapping Church and Ministry plus Cultural Intelligence

Introduction

The discussions and examples presented throughout this book have tried to demonstrate the significance of cultural intelligence in missions and ministries. Cultural intelligence encompasses what drives us to interact with other cultures (motivation), what we know about cultural patterns and behaviours (knowledge), how we plan and monitor our cross–cultural interactions (strategy) and how we actually interact with others in cross-cultural missions and ministries (behaviour). Through a mix of genetics and the environment in which we grew up, some of us naturally excel in these various areas of CQ, like James Bond and the Apostle Paul. But the majority of us, I suspect, could use some work in several of these areas. Between the increasing global nature of our society, and the impetus to share the Gospel message with others, improving our CQ is not just something that would be nice to do, it is a real necessity if we are to succeed in missions and ministries. Here below is a snapshot of some general ways in which we can adopt or practice cultural intelligence in missions and ministries, as well as in other facets of our lives.

Start Small

Whenever we face a monumental task, we often become overwhelmed at the prospect, which prevents us from even starting in the first place. A good place to start is with our own family. Does my spouse or do my in-laws come from a different cultural background? What about my sister-in-law or uncle? Most of us have a family large enough that we do not have to go far to find ethnic and cultural diversity. And for this purpose, the closer the better. However, it might be good to note that for many, this might not be the case, especially for those in an individualist culture, where families are very small units or where there are no intermarriages. Now the question becomes, what concrete steps have I taken to understand the culture that forms such an integral part of their identity? If they are bilingual and have spent years learning English, have I spent any time learning at least a few words or phrases in their native language? Have I read about some of the broader characteristics and belief systems of that culture and talked with them about how those values still ring true, or how they have changed their values or beliefs with exposure to another culture?

Improving Cultural Intelligence in the Workplace

Most of the literature related to CQ focuses on the business world. As international executives operate their businesses in more diverse cultures, it is vital that they understand the values and ideals of each culture, while staying away from any cultural taboos. But even if we are not some business executive signing international deals over breakfast, there are still many benefits that we can glean from improving our CQ. Do we have co-workers from different cultures or regular customers or clients with whom we interact who come from different cultural backgrounds? It is often tempting to simply adopt the mindset that since we are in the United Kingdom, individuals from other cultures have the responsibility to learn our cultural norms and expectations, and our only responsibility is to teach them these norms and expectations when they break them.

But what a shift it would be if we could learn from our customers, clients, or co-workers; if we learned to ask about their background and upbringing, and if we adopted the role of cultural student, rather than cultural teacher. Obviously, such conversations are not always appropriate, but in many instances they could be. Displaying a true interest in someone else's roots shows a level of care and concern for others that draws them in. In a business setting, customers and clients want to feel valued by those with whom they do business. Deepening such social connections in a business setting is good for business. It is the same in our church settings, where social connections and community are important.

Cultural Literacy and Bible Study

Throughout this book, we have continually called attention to examples of cultural intelligence within the biblical text itself. But in so doing, in some instances, it became clear that the original readers of the biblical text had a certain cultural literacy that we do not share. This was the situation with the legal issues surrounding a kinsman-redeemer in Ruth and the biological worldview apparent in Paul's letter to the Corinthians. The idea of cultural literacy was expressed most clearly by E. D. Hirsch, Jr., a professor of English at the University of Virginia. He published a book entitled *Cultural Literacy: What Every American Needs to Know*. In writing this book, Hirsch scoured popular books, newspaper articles, and television shows in order to identify assumed cultural knowledge on the part of the audience. In his appendix, he lists around five thousand items that constitute cultural events, heroes, biblical characters, and geographical terms that writers simply refer to without any further explanation. They assume that the average American knows these terms and what they convey. This list would be different for the United Kingdom (but would obviously include some overlap).

When we study the Bible, we are reading books that were written for an audience with a completely different set of cultural references and knowledge. The task of pastors, biblical scholars, and theologians is often to identify those assumed cultural references that are not spelled out in the biblical text itself. Without knowledge of such references, we can either fail to understand or misunderstand the message that the inspired biblical writers were conveying. When we interact with the Bible, we are in essence in a cross-cultural setting. Taking the time to learn about the Israelite and Greek cultures will help us to further understand the biblical world and the message found within these stories, letters and psalms.

Passing on Cultural Intelligence

By far, the foundations of a strong CQ lie in the experiences we had in our childhood. The more cross-cultural experience we grew up with, the higher our CQ will likely be. So as parents, or future parents, how do we give our children the best chance of thriving in our global world? It starts with our own attitudes towards cross-cultural situations. Our children pick up on and often adopt the attitudes that we express toward different situations. If we take the time to make cross-cultural interaction a conscious part of our awareness, we can then model for our children the value of intercultural interaction. We can take the time to teach them about different values and cultural expectations or taboos with which we are familiar and increase their cultural knowledge.

Cultural Intelligence in Our Church Community

Our church community is intentionally both ethnically and culturally diverse. As a community, we value the insights that we can gain from interacting closely with individuals from other cultures. But we don't want this interaction to be kept at arm's length. We desire an integrated church community, where members from various cultures are connected through our shared love of Jesus Christ. As we love one another, as Christ loved the church, we want that spirit of love and community to be evident within our church and to be evident to the wider community of which we are a part.

It is important that we continue to think of ways to celebrate the cultural heritage and diversity within our congregation. Not only that, but our theology should be such that it is not just tied to English or even

Western culture. African and Asian theologians often bring insights to religious discussions that do not occur to Western theologians. If we are to truly acknowledge the global nature of the Church and of the Gospel, we must no longer be content with a theology that is tied so closely to English culture (see our documentary video, entitled "From Theology2theologies").

One such example from theological discourse appears in liberation theology. This theological movement emerged in South America in the 1950s and moved in the 1960s to Africa, where it has flourished. Liberation theology emphasizes the necessity for Christians, who have come to know God and his redemptive character, to oppose social and political injustice (Ilesanmi, 1995). In Western society, we typically talk of divorcing politics from religion and remaining apolitical in our church community. The South American and African perspectives expressed in liberation theology declare that such a division is impossible in light of the Gospel message, which urges us to care for the poor and to identify with their suffering. When we see social injustice, it is not enough to simply pray for those suffering under such injustice; we are called to be proactive, socially and politically, to stop such injustice where it arises. This is not to say that we must adopt liberation theology or other African or Asian theological systems, but we should certainly take seriously the critiques which they present to our own theological system and be willing to adjust our theology in light of such critiques.

Summary

Developing a high CQ will involve training our heart (motivational), mind (knowledge), and body (action). We need to take careful stock of our attitudes and self-confidence, our general and specific cultural knowledge, as well as our ability to speak and behave in such a way that we express love to those from different cultures, rather than aloofness or disdain. We can start small and move out from there. As with any area of our life, we will not be perfect; we will make mistakes. But by continuing to take risks and to actively participate in cross-cultural events, we will find our self-confidence growing, along with our competence. This in turn should encourage us to seek further such interactions, creating an upward spiral. As we engage in such activities, we model for our children what healthy cross-cultural behaviour looks like. It should also help to inspire our family, friends, and co-workers to seek similar activities and interactions.

Discussion Questions

1) Can you name two things that you learned from this class that you did not know before?

2) Are there one or two practical applications of CQ that you hope to implement in the coming weeks or months?

3) Using your imagination, share what you think a culturally competent church might look like.

4) Discuss what you believe Jesus would do in a very diverse cultural setting like London.

RESULTS

Scripture warns us not only to be hearers of the Word but also to be doers of the Word. As you spend time living out some of the principles learnt in this chapter, write out below a reflection on how you apply them to practical issues. When the group comes together next time, consider sharing with each other your experiences.

About the Author

Osoba Otaigbe is an accredited Baptist minister with the Baptist Union of Great Britain and also an Advanced CQ Certified Facilitator by the Cultural Intelligence Centre. Over the past thirty years, Osoba has been in cross-cultural leadership positions with eighteen years as an entrepreneur within the oil and gas industry. Osoba has also served twelve years in two London Baptist Churches (Tooting Junction Baptist Church and Memorial Community Church). Apart from that, he also served as the chair of the London Baptist Association Mission Strategy Forum. The forum serves as the strategic mission think-tank of the association and seeks to facilitate creative, innovative and pioneering approaches to mission in cross-cultural places and spaces where local churches may not be best placed to respond for a variety of reasons. He studied Business, Computer Science and later on Theology. Osoba now brings his thirty years of experience in business and as a mission strategist to the world of intercultural competence consulting and coaching.

Bibliography

Chapter 1

P. Christopher Earley and Soon Ang. 2003. *Cultural Intelligence: Individual Interactions across Cultures*: Stanford, California.

Chapter 2

Livermore, David. 2011. *The Cultural Intelligence Difference: Master the One Skill You Can't Do Without in Today's Global Economy.* New York.

Chapter 3

Ryan, Richard M., and Edward L. Deci. 1985. *Intrinsic Motivation and Self-Determination in Human Behavior.* Springer Science & Business Media.

Ryan, Richard M., and Edward L. Deci. 2000. Intrinsic and extrinsic motivations: Classic definitions and new directions. *Contemporary Educational Psychology* 25: 54–67.

Ryan, Richard M., and Edward L. Deci. 2008. Self-determination theory: A macrotheory of human motivation, development, and health. *Canadian Psychology* 49 (3): 182–85.

Chapter 4

Furham, Adrian, Tatsuro Hosoe, and Thomas Li-Ping Tang. 2001. Male hubris and female humility? A cross-cultural study of ratings of self, parental, and sibling multiple intelligence in America, Britain, and Japan. *Intelligence 30*: 101–115.

Chapter 5

Ghonsooly, Behzad, and Somayye Shalchy. 2013. Cultural intelligence and writing ability: Delving into fluency, accuracy and complexity. *Novitas-ROYAL (Research on Youth and Language)* 7(2): 147–159.

Livermore, David. 2011. *The Cultural Intelligence Difference: Master the One Skill You Can't Do Without in Today's Global Economy.* New York.

http://www.tlu.ee/~sirvir/Leadership/Leadership%20Dimensions/ globe_project.html Accessed on May 13, 2015

Chapter 7

Livermore, David. 2011. *The Cultural Intelligence Difference: Master the One Skill You Can't Do Without in Today's Global Economy.* New York.

Chapter 8

Livermore, David. 2011. *The Cultural Intelligence Difference: Master the One Skill You Can't Do Without in Today's Global Economy.* New York.

Middleton, Julie. 2014. "What Is Cultural Intelligence?" http://commonpurpose.org/knowledge-hub/all-articles/what-is-cultural-intelligence (Accessed April 13, 2015).

Rockstuhl, Thomas, Ying-Yi Hong, Kok Yee Ng, Soon Ang, and Chi-Yue Chiu. 2010. The culturally intelligent brain: From detecting to bridging cultural differences. *NeuroLeadership Journal 3*: 1–15.

Thomas, David C. 2006. Domain and development of cultural intelligence: The importance of mindfulness. *Group and Organization Management 31*, 1: 78–99.

Chapter 9

Campbell, Edward F. 1964. *Ruth*. New York.

Livermore, David. 2011. *The Cultural Intelligence Difference: Master the One Skill You Can't Do Without in Today's Global Economy*. New York.

Pope, Marvin H. 1992. "Euphemism and Dysphemism in the Bible," in David Noel Freedman (ed.), *The Anchor Bible Dictionary*, pp. 720–725. New York.

Chapter 10

Bernard, Phyllis E. 2009. Bringing soul to international negotiation. *Negotiation Journal*, 147–159. 6th April, 2009

Livermore, David. 2011. *The Cultural Intelligence Difference: Master the One Skill You Can't Do Without in Today's Global Economy*. New York.

Chapter 11

Martin, Troy W. 2004. Paul's argument from nature for the veil in 1 Corinthians 11:13–15: A testicle instead of a head covering. *Journal of Biblical Literature 123*: 75–84.

Mehrabian, Albert. 1971. *Silent Messages*. Wadsworth Publishing Co.

Morrison, Terri, Wayne Conaway, and George Borden. 1994. *Kiss, Bow, or Shake Hands*. Bob Adams Inc.

Oster, Richard. 1988. When men wore veils to worship: The historical context of 1 Corinthians 11.4. *New Testament Studies 34*: 481–505.

Thompson, Cynthia L. 1988. Hairstyles, head-coverings, and St. Paul: Portraits from Roman Corinth. *Biblical Archaeologist 51*: 99–115.

Van Dyne, Linn, Soon Ang, Kok Yee Ng, Thomas Rockstuhl, Mei Ling Tan, and Christine Koh. 2012. Sub-dimensions of the four-factor model of cultural intelligence: Expanding the conceptualization and measurement of cultural intelligence. *Social and Personality Psychology Compass 6* (4): 295–313.

Chapter 12

Hirsch, E. D. 1987. *Cultural Literacy: What Every American Needs to Know.* Houghton Mifflin.

Ilesanmi, Simeon O. 1995. Inculturation and liberation: Christian social ethics and the African Theology Project. *Annal of the Society of Christian Ethics 15*: 49–73.

Printed in the United States
By Bookmasters